The Complete Illustrated

THORBURN'S BIRDS

The Complete Illustrated

THORBURN'S BIRDS

Illustrated by
ARCHIBALD THORBURN

with an Introduction and Notes by
Peter J.S. Olney

BEAVER
PUBLISHING

This edition published in Great Britain by
Beaver Publishing Limited
Alderley Edge, Cheshire, SK9 7DT.1997

Beaver Publishing is an imprint of Ravette Publishing limited

ISBN 1 85962 056 6

© Wordsworth Editions Limited 1997

Wordsworth® is a registered trade mark of
Wordsworth Editions Limited

Designed by Robert Mathias, Publishing Workshop

Printed and bound by
Artes Graficas Elkar, Bilbao, Spain

INTRODUCTION

Archibald Thorburn, painter and natural history book illustrator, was born May 31 1860 at Lasswade, Midlothian and died October 9 1935 at Hascombe, Surrey. His father, Robert Thorburn, was in his time an admired miniaturist painter, who encouraged and coached his talented son. Notwithstanding Archibald's formal education in Dalkeith and Edinburgh and at art school in London, he always acknowledged his debt to his father's tuition. His earliest compositions were flower pictures and landscapes but his favourite subjects were birds, his interest being not only as an artist but also as a keen sportsman and field-observer.

He rarely used oils, painting almost entirely in water-colours, supplemented with flake-white for special effects. His landscapes combine a sense of composition, tone and colour and a deeply emotional response to nature, while his subjects, most often birds and mammals, are painted with accuracy and yet give a realistic impression of the living animal. His gift was to combine artistic flair with scientific precision. Simple pencil sketches caught the natural stance of his subject, and beautiful, unpretentious water colours provided accurate information on plumage and body colours. He used his observations of the animal in the wild and living specimens in zoos and private collections; for finer detail he often used skins. Thorburn was among the first to break away from the draughtman's fashion of illustrating birds merely as a flat scientific map of plumage. His birds are essentially solid, living creatures, placed in their natural environment.

His first published work was two uncoloured pictures in 1883 in Edmund Harting's *Sketches of bird-life*, but his first major assignment was for Walter Swaysland's *Familiar wild birds* (1883-88, four volumes) in which over one hundred of the bird plates are the first coloured reproductions of Thorburn's water-colour drawings. It was however, his contribution to Lord Lilford's *Coloured figures of the birds of the British Islands* (1885-98, seven volumes), for which he produced nearly two-thirds of the 421 chromolithograph plates, which brought him wide recognition. Thorburn began work for Lord Lilford in 1887 and over the next ten years completed 268 paintings, following detailed instructions (and some criticism) by Lilford who required absolute accuracy in colour, posture and plumage. Lilford's exacting demands were excellent training for Thorburn who used his own field knowledge and landscape painting abilities to produce pictures which were accurate and aesthetically pleasing.

By the turn of the century Thorburn's reputation was well established and he was in great demand as an illustrator of sporting and natural history books and as a painter for exhibition and for private customers. Thorburn eventually wrote and illustrated four titles of his own: British birds (1915- 1918), *A naturalist's sketch book* (1919), *British Mammal* (1920-21) and *Game birds and wild-fowl of Great Britain and Ireland* (1923). In these books he could choose to work to his own designs and this freedom is reflected in his individualistic approach to the composition of plates and text. His *British Birds* was published in a fourth edition in 1925-26) in new octavo format in four volumes, each with 48 new colour plates, as opposed to the 20 in each of the four volumes of the first edition.

He was a lifelong supporter and a Vice President of the Royal Society for the Protection of Birds and following a suggestion from the owner of his London gallery he frequently painted for the Society a picture to be used for their Christmas card. He drew, without fee, the designs for the 1899, 1905, 1916-19, and 1923-35 cards as a token of his admiration for the work of the Society and to help protect the birds which he had enjoyed watching and painting. Thorburn's picture for the 1935 card was of a goldcrest, which he did when lying in bed during his last painful illness. His last book illustrations were published posthumously in Archer's and Godman's *Birds of British Somaliland and the Gulf of Aden* (1937

Thorburn's working life spanned the period of the last blossoming of hand-coloured lithography through to the invention of chromolithography and letterpress colour reproduction. The development of modern printing processes, with their much more durable printing plates, revolutionised the production of colour plates, making them much cheaper to reproduce in book form and consequently more accessible to the general public.

He was painting at a time when there was an increasing demand for books with illustrations of the living animal rather than those based only on museum specimens; illustrations which could be used to identify and provide some idea of the animal's normal habitat; illustrations which satisfied the field and armchair naturalist. It is a testimony to his talent that his illustrations and paintings are still appreciated and in demand.

BRITISH BIRDS

British Birds was originally published in four quarto volumes, the 1st edition 1915 (volumes 1 and 2), 1916 (volumes 3 and 4) and 1918 (supplement), the 2nd edition 1916-1918, and the 3rd edition 1917 (volumes 1 and 2 only; volumes 3 and 4 with an adjusted print order). Thorburn adopted the classification and nomenclature of Howard Saunder's, *An illustrated Manual of British Birds*, 2nd edition, 1899. London: Gurney and Jackson, with a number of changes 'to suit the requirements of the plates'. Saunder's arrangement of bird families and species largely followed 'The list of British Birds compiled by a commitee of the British Ornithologists' Union', which at that time had the order Passeriformes at the begining as being the most specialised of birds and a sequence of families which differs from that commonly used now.

For his *Britsh Birds* Thorburn tried to represent as many species as possible of the same family on the same plate and drawn to the same scale. The stance, colours and plumage shows that he was an excellent observer and the hint of habitat he gave accurately reflects the environment of the bird. He included all the then-resident species and most of those species which more or less regularly, or even rarely, visited Britain. He figured 407 species, of which a small number have since been rejected from the British-Irish List after a re-examination of the original data. In good faith he included six species of the now notorious 'Hastings Rarities', which were said to have been observed or collected between 1892 and 1930 in the Hastings area of east Sussex and west Kent. The circumstances surrounding the recording of the so-called 'Hasting Rarities' were critically analysed by E.M.Nicholson and I.J.Ferguson-Lees, British Birds (1962) 55:299-384, and their recommendations for deletions and further re-examination were accepted by the British Ornithologists' Union Records Committee and Council (Ibis (1963) 105: 289-291. Six species and 13 subspecies (races) were deleted from the official British-Irish List and the status of a larger number of scarce species was also affected.

The BOU Records Committee's Twenty-third Report, Ibis, (1997) 139: 197-201, states that there are now 550 species on the official British and Irish List, of which six have been recorded only in Ireland.

ORGANISATION OF NEW TEXT

Though it is now superseded the arrangement of families and species has been left as in Thorburn's original publication but the opportunity has been taken to provide a completely new summary text giving up-to-date information.

The organisation of the text is:
- generally accepted English name, and in brackets the name given by Thorburn if different
- the scentific name and in brackets the scientific name given by Thorburn if different
- range or median of total length
- basic information on breeding and non-breeding distribution
- main generalised habitat requirements
- main food items
- status of the species based primarily on the categories (see addendum 1) in the *Checklist of Birds of Britain and Ireland* (6th edition, 1992) and the subsequent reports of the BOU Records Committee, up to the 23rd Report (July 1996, published 1997). Those species in the UK Red list and those of Global Conservation Concern are also noted (see Addendum 2)
- in parenthesis english name and scientific name if different from the generally accepted names (i.e., in Sibley and Monroe, 1990 and 1993, Monroe and Sibley 1993, and /or in the 1992 *BOU Checklist*)

For greater detail the reader should consult the addenda and bibliography given at the end of the text.

PETER J.S.OLNEY
August 1997

CONTENTS

ADDENDA   10

BIBLIOGRAPHY   12

THE PLATES   13

NOTES ON THE PLATES   97

INDEX TO PLATES   127

ADDENDA

ADDENDUM 1

The list of birds recorded in Britain and Ireland is maintained by the British Ornithologists' Union through its Records Committttee. The first checklist was published in 1883 and the last list, the sixth edition of the Checklist of Birds of Britain and Ireland, was published in 1992. Taxonomy and status are reassessed as an ongoing process and additions and corrections to the checklist are published in the BOU's journal Ibis in regular updated reports. The checklist and subsequent reports have been followed in the text. The status of each species in the text follows that of the checklist and uses the same coding:

RB: Resident breeder
MB: Migrant breeder
IB: Introduced breeder
CB: Casual breeder
FB: Former breeder
WV: Winter visitor
PV: Passage visitor
SV: Scarce visitor

Some of these codes are only generalisations and need some clarification. For example, many forms listed as WV may occasionally occur in summer. RB and MB together imply that the species is a partial migrant in which a proportion of the population leaves Britain and Ireland in winter. CB includes those forms that nest less than annually and those where there are fewer than 10 breeding attempts each year. SV is kept for those rare taxa for which descriptions are required by the British Birds Rarities Committee, and for some of the rarer races not usually identifiable in the field. A small number of PVs are rarer than some SVs.

ADDENDUM 2

Species in Thorburn's British Birds which are now of conservation concern

Species of Global Conservation Concern

Capped petrel *Pterodroma hasitata* (EN)
Red-breasted goose *Branta ruficollis* (VU)
Ferruginous duck *Aythya nyroca* (VU)
Steller's eider *Polysticta stelleri* (VU)
Spotted eagle *Aquila clanga* (VU)
Lesser kestrel *Falco naumanni* (VU)
Corncrake *Crex crex* (VU)
Great bustard *Otis tarda* (VU)
Sociable plover *Vanellus gregaria* (VU)
Aquatic warbler *Acrocephalus paludicola* (VU)
Scottish crossbill *Loxia scotica* (VU)

(EN) = Endangered. (VU) = Vulnerable. IUCN threat categories from Collar, N.J., Crosby, M.J., & Stattersfield, A.J. (1994): *Birds to Watch 2: The World List of Threatened Birds*. Cambridge: Birdlife International.

UK Red Listed Species of High Conservation Concern

Bittern *Botaurus stellaris*
Common Scoter *Melanitta nigra*
Red Kite *Milvus milvus*
White-tailed Eagle *Haliaeetus albicilla*
Marsh Harrier *Circus aeruginosus*
Hen Harrier *Circus cyaneus*
Osprey *Pandion haliaetus*
Merlin *Falco columbarius*
Black Grouse *Tetrao tetrix*
Capercaillie *Tetrao urogallus*
Grey Partridge *Perdix perdix*
Quail *Coturnix coturnix*
Corncrake *Crex crex**
Stone-curlew *Burhinus oedicnemus*
Black-tailed Godwit *Limosa limosa*
Red-necked Phalarope *Phalaropus fulicarius*
Roseate Tern *Sterna Sterna dougallii*
Turtle Dove *Streptopelia turtur*
Nightjar *Caprimulgus europaeus*
Wryneck *Jynx torquilla*
Woodlark *Lullula arborea*
Skylark *Alauda arvensis*
Song Thrush *Turdus philomelos*
Aquatic Warbler *Acrocephalus paludicola**
Marsh Warbler *Acrocephalus palustris*
Dartford Warbler *Sylvia undata*
Spotted Flycatcher *Muscicapa striata*
Red-backed Shrike *Lanius collurio*
Tree Sparrow *Passer montanus*
Linnet *Carduelis cannabina*
Twite *Carduelis flavirostris*
Scottish Crossbill *Loxia scotica**
Bullfinch *Pyrrhula pyrrhula*
Cirl Bunting *Emberiza cirlus*
Reed Bunting *Emberiza schoeniclus*
Corn Bunting *Miliaria calandra*

UK Red list species are those whose population or range is rapidly declining, recently or historically, and those of global conservation concern: these species are of the greatest conservation concern and deserve urgent, effective conservation action. *Birds of Conservation Concern in the UK, Channel Islands and Isle of Man* (1996). Sandy, Beds: RSPB.

* Species also of Global Conservation Concern.

ADDENDUM 3

Distribution
Distribution is given in general terms, as breeding range, followed by non-breeding range, if different from breeding range, omitting casual vagrants.
For the sake of brevity, I have sometimes used the names of zoogeographical regions rather than continental or country names.

Boundaries between regions, especially in the transitional zones, are sometimes approximate but even so regions remain a convenient aid in describing distribution.

Most authorities use the same or similar boundaries in defining regions and their subdivisions, but there are sometimes confusing differences in these definitions. For the sake of clarity I have used the following terms based on those employed by Sibley and Monroe (1990):

NEARCTIC – North America together with a portion of nontropical Mexico

NEOTROPICAL – Central and South America south of the Nearctic region

NORTH AMERICA – areas north of Mexico and the West Indies

MIDDLE AMERICA – Mexico and Central America

WEST INDIES – Greater Antilles, Lesser Antilles, Bahamas and small Caribbean islands.

PALEARCTIC – the boundaries are broadly defined in the west, north and east by the Atlantic, Arctic and Pacific oceans, separating it from the Nearctic, and in the south extending into Africa north of the Sahara, or the eastern Atlantic islands but excluding the Oriental region.

EURASIA – the continental landmass

AFRICA – the continental landmass

AFRICAN REGION – includes the portion of the Ethiopian area of the southern Arabian peninsula, Madagascar and other nearby islands

AFROTROPICAL REGION – Africa south of the Sahara, excluding Madagascar and the Comoro islands

ORIENTAL REGION – tropical Asia and western Indonesia

SOUTHERN ASIA – Indian subcontinent and southern China plus southeastern Asian area, more or less equivalent to the Oriental region

SOUTHEAST ASIA – region from Burma, Thailand and Indochina south to the Greater Sunda Islands (except Sulawesi); biologically it includes extreme eastern India and extreme southwestern China.

EAST INDIES – here restricted to Greater and Lesser Sunda Islands plus the Moluccas.

MALAY ARCHIPELAGO – East Indies plus the Philippines.

AUSTRALIAN REGION – Australia plus New Guinea

NEW GUINEA REGION – New Guinea plus adjacent western Papuan islands and Bismarck Archipelago.

AUSTRALASIAN REGION – eastern Indonesia, New Guinea, Australia, New Zealand and islands in adjacent areas (east to Solomon Islands)

SOUTHERN ASIA, MALAY ARCHIPELAGO AND AUSTRALASIA – Oriental and Australian regions

INDIA – includes Nepal and Bhutan, also Bangladesh and Sri Lanka

OCEANIA – divided into Micronesia, Polynesia and Melanesia, but the Hawaiian Islands are kept separate

BIBLIOGRAPHY

British Ornithologists Union (1992): *Checklist of Birds of Britain and Ireland. 6th Edition.* Tring, Herts: British Ornithologists' Union.

British Ornitholgists' Union Records Committee's Reports: 17th Report, May 1992 (1992) Ibis 134: 380-381; 18th Report, December 1992 (1993) Ibis 135: 220-222; 19th Report, May 1993 (1993) Ibis 135: 493-499; 20th Report, December 1993 (1994) Ibis 136: 253-255; 21st Report, May 1994 (1994) Ibis 136: 497; 22nd Report, May 1995 (1995) Ibis 137: 590-591; 23rd Report, July 1996 (1997) *Ibis* 139: 197-201.

Cramp, S & Simmonds, K.E.L. (eds.) (1977, 1980,& 1983): The *Birds of the Western Palearctic*, Vols.I, II, & III. Oxford: Oxford University Press.

Cramp, S. (ed.) (1985, 1988, & 1992): *The Birds of the Western Palearctic.* Vols. IV, V, & VI. Oxford: Oxford University Press.

Cramp, S & Perrins, C.M.(eds.) (1993, 1994 & 1994): *The Birds of the Western Palearctic.* Vols. VII, VIII, & IX. Oxford: Oxford University Press.

Collar, N.J., Crosby, M.J. & Stattersfield, A.J. (1994): *Birds to Watch: The World List of Threatened Birds.* Cambridge: Birdlife International.

Dymond, J.N., Fraser, P.A. & Gantlett, S.J.M. (1989): *Rare birds in Britain and Ireland.* Calton: T.& A.D.Poyser.

Gladstone, H.S. (1936): Obituary Archibald Thorburn. *Scot. Naturalist* **217**: 1-7.

Heredia, B., Rose, L. & Painter, M. (1996): *Globally threatened birds in Europe: Action plans.* Strasbourg: Council of Europe Publishing.

Jackson, C.E. (1975): *Bird Illustrators.* London: H.F.Witherby Ltd.

Lodge, G.E.L. (1935): Obituary Archibald Thorburn. *Brit. Birds* **29**: 172.

Lodge, G.E.L. (1936): Obituary Archibald Thorburn. *Ibis* 13th Ser. **6**: 205-207.

Marchant, J.H., Hudson, R., Carter, S.P. & Whittington, P. (1990): *Population trends in British breeding birds.* Tring: British Trust for Ornithology.

Monroe, B.L. & Sibley, C.G. (1993): *A World Checklist of Birds.* New Haven and London: Yale University Press.

Sibley, C.G. & Monroe, B.L. (1990): *Distribution and Taxonomy of Birds of the World.* New Haven and London: Yale University Press.

Sibley, C.G. & Monroe, B.L. (1993): *A Supplement to Distribution and Taxonomy of Birds of the World.* New Haven and London: Yale University Press.

Stone, B.H., Sears, J., Cranswick, P.A., Gregory, R.D., Gibbons, D.W., Rehfisch, M.M., Aebischer, N.J., & Reid, J.B. (1997): *Population estimates of birds in Britain and in the United Kingdom. Brit. Birds* **90**: 1-22.

Tucker, G.M. & Heath, M.F. (1994): *Birds in Europe: Their Conservation Status.* Cambridge: Birdlife International.

THE PLATES

Pl. 1.

Archibald Thorburn
1915

Mistle-Thrush

Black-Throated Thrush
♂ & ♀.

Song-Thrush

Fieldfare

Redwing

Pl. 2

A. Thorburn
1913

Siberian Thrush White's Thrush Dusky Thrush
Ring-Ouzel   Blackbird   Rock Thrush

Pl. 5.

Wheatear ♂ & ♀

Desert Wheatear

Eastern Stonechat

Pied Wheatear

Isabelline Wheatear

Black-throated & Black-eared Wheatear

Black Wheatear

Stonechat

Pl.4

Redstart   Redbreast

Black Redstart   Whinchat   Nightingale

White-spotted Bluethroat   Arctic Bluethroat

Archibald Thorburn 1915

Pl. 5.

Whitethroat
Blackcap
♂ & ♀
Barred Warbler
Thrush-Nightingale

Lesser Whitethroat
Orphean Warbler
Sardinian Warbler
Garden-Warbler

2/3

Pl. 6.

Subalpine Warbler.

Dartford Warbler.   Willow-Wren.

Wood-Wren

Yellow-browed Warbler

Pallas's Willow Warbler

Greenish Willow-Warbler

Chiffchaff.

Pl. 7

Melodious Warbler.   Icterine Warbler.
Rufous Warbler.   Radde's Bush-Warbler.
Marsh-Warbler.   Reed Warbler.

Pl. 8.

Sedge-Warbler   Savi's Warbler
Cetti's Warbler   Great Reed-Warbler   Aquatic Warbler
              Grasshopper-Warbler

Pl. 9

Archibald Thorburn
1913.

Goldcrest
Firecrest   Nuthatch
        Wren   Hedge-Sparrow
    Alpine Accentor.   Dipper

2/3

Pl. 10.

Marsh-Titmouse.   Long-tailed Titmouse.

Great Titmouse.   Bearded Titmouse.
                                        ♂ & ♀

Coal-Titmouse.   Crested Titmouse. Blue Titmouse.

Pl. 11.

Wall Creeper (summer & winter)   Tree-Creeper
        Pied Wagtail.   Blue-headed Wagtail.
   White Wagtail   Grey Wagtail.
Grey-headed Yellow Wagtail.   Yellow Wagtail.

Pl. 12.

Rock Pipit.
Tawny Pipit.
Meadow-Pipit.

Richard's Pipit.

Tree-Pipit.
Red-throated Pipit.
Alpine Pipit.

2/3

Pl. 13.

Red-backed Shrike. ♂ & ♀.   Great Grey Shrike

Woodchat Shrike.   Masked Shrike   Lesser Grey Shrike

Pl. 14

Waxwing.   Spotted Flycatcher.

Red-breasted Flycatcher.

Pied Flycatcher.

Collared Flycatcher. Golden Oriole

Brown Flycatcher

2

Pl. 15.

Red-rumped Swallow.   Sand-Martin.
Swallow.   Siskin.   Martin.
Goldfinch.   Hawfinch.   Greenfinch.

Pl. II

Mealy Redpoll.   Serin.
Lesser Redpoll.   Citril Finch.   Linnet.
Brambling (Summer & Winter)   Tree Sparrow.
Chaffinch.   House Sparrow (♂ & ♀)

Pl. 17.

Corn Bunting.
Black-headed Bunting.
Bullfinch ♂♀♀.

Twite.
Pine-Bunting.
Two-barred Crossbill.
—Crossbill.

Snow-Finch.
Scarlet Grosbeak.
Pine-Grosbeak.

Pl.

Rustic Bunting.   Little Bunting.   Yellow Bunting or Yellow Hammer.
Cirl Bunting.   Yellow-breasted Bunting.   Reed Bunting.   Lapland Bunting.
Siberian Meadow Bunting. Meadow-Bunting.   Snow-Bunting.
Ortolan.   (Summer & Autumn.)

Pl. 19.

Starling. (summer & winter)

Nutcracker

Jay.

Rose-coloured Starling.

(adult & young)

Chough.

Pl. 20

Magpie.   Raven.   Jackdaw.

Pl. 21.

Carrion Crow. Rook. Hooded Crow.

Pl. 22

Sky-Lark.

Shore-Lark.

Crested Lark

Wood Lark

Short-toed Lark.

White-winged Lark.

Black Lark (summer & winter)

Pl. 23.

Swift   Needle-tailed Swift. Nightjar.

Red-necked Nightjar.   Egyptian Nightjar.   Alpine Swift.

Pl. 24

Wryneck.   Green Woodpecker.
Lesser Spotted Woodpecker ♂♀.   Great Spotted Woodpecker (adult ♂♀ & young)
          Kingfisher.   Roller.

Pl. 25.

Cuckoo. (adult & young).   Great Spotted Cuckoo
American Yellow-billed Cuckoo.   Bee-eater.   Hoopoe.

4/9

Pl. 26

Long-eared Owl.

Barn-Owl

Tawny Owl.

Short-eared Owl.

Pl. 27

Hawk-Owl.   Scops Owl.

Tengmalm's Owl (with Dusky Warbler)

Snowy Owl. ♂   Little Owl.

Pl. 2.

Eagle Owl.

Pl. 29.

A. Thorburn
1914

Griffon-Vulture
Egyptian Vulture. (adult & young)

Pl. 36

Montagu's Harrier. ♂ & ♀.　　Marsh-Harrier. (adult ♂ & young)　　Hen-Harrier. ♂ & ♀.

Pl. 31.

Rough-legged Buzzard.   Spotted Eagle.   Common Buzzard

Pl. 32

Golden Eagle (adult & young)

A. Thorburn 1914

Pl. 33.

A. Thorburn
1914.

White-tailed or Sea Eagle.
(adult & young)

Osprey.

Pl. 3.

A. Thorburn 1914

Sparrow-Hawk. (♂ & ♀)

Goshawk (adult & young)

Pl. 35.

Black Kite.

Kite.

Honey-Buzzard. (2 varieties)

Pl. 3

A. Thorburn. 1914

Greenland Falcon. ♀   Iceland Falcon. ♂

Pl. 37.

Gyr-Falcon.
♀.

Peregrine Falcon (adult & young).
♂.

⅓.

Pl. 38

Hobby. ♂.

Merlin (♂, ♀ & young).   Kestrel ♀.

Red-footed Falcon (♂ & ♀).

Lesser Kestrel ♂.

Kestrel ♂.

Pl. 39

Gannet. (adults & young)

Cormorant. (adult & young)

Shag. (adult & young)

Pl. 40.

A. Thorburn 1914

Buff-backed Heron.

Little Egret.

Common Heron.

Purple Heron.

Great White Heron

Pl. 41

Night-Heron

Glossy Ibis.   Little Bittern.   Squacco Heron.
Common Bittern.   American Bittern.

Pl. 42

Spoonbill.

White Stork.

Flamingo.

Black Stork.

$\frac{1}{6}$

Pl. 43

White-fronted Goose.
Pink-footed Goose.

Grey Lag-Goose,
Bean-Goose.

4.

Brent Goose.
Red-breasted Goose.

Bernacle Goose.
Snow Goose.

Pl. 45.

Bewick's Swan.   Whooper Swan.
Mute Swan (adult & young).

Pl.46.

Mallard (♂&♀)
Ruddy Sheld-Duck.

Gadwall. (♂&♀)
Common Sheld-Duck.

Pl. 41

Teal. (♂♀) Shoveller (♂♀)
American Blue-winged Teal. (♂♀). American Green-winged Teal
Pintail. (♂♀)

3

Pl. 4.

Pochard. (♂♀)

American Wigeon. (♂♀)

Wigeon. (♂♀)

Red-crested Pochard. (♂♀)

Garganey. (♂♀)

Pl. 49.

Tufted Duck. (♂ ♀)   Ferruginous Duck. (♂ ♀)
Buffel-headed Duck. (♂ ♀)   Golden-eye. (♂ ♀)   Scaup-Duck. (♂ ♀)
Long-tailed Duck. (♂ ♀)

Pl. 50.

Harlequin Duck (♂&♀)

King-Eider. (♂&♀)

Eider Duck. (♂&♀)

3.

Pl. 57

Surf. Scoter (♂&♀),   Steller's Eider (♂&♀)

Common Scoter (♂&♀),   Velvet Scoter (♂&♀).

Pl. 5

Red-breasted Merganser.(♂&♀)
Goosander.(♂&♀)
Hooded Merganser.(♂&♀)
Smew.(♂&♀)

Pl. 53.

Wood Pigeon.   Stock Dove.
Turtle Dove. Pallas's Sand-Grouse. (♂ & ♀)   Rock Dove.

⅓

Pl. 54

A. Thorburn. 1915.

Capercaillie ($ & ♀)

Pl. 55.

A. Thorburn. 1915.

Red Grouse. (♂ & ♀).
Black Grouse. (♂ & ♀).

Pl. 56

A. Thorburn
1915

Ptarmigan (♂ & ♀): winter & autumn.

Pl. 57.

Mongolian Pheasant. (♂&♀).   Pheasant. (♂&♀).   Japanese Pheasant.(♂)
Chinese Ring-necked Pheasant. (♂).

Pl. 58

Common Partridge. (♂ & ♀)

Red-legged Partridge. (♂ & ♀)

Quail. (♂ & ♀)

⅓

Pl. 59.

Coot.

Moor-hen.   Water-Rail.   Carolina Crake. Spotted Crake.

Baillon's Crake.   Little Crake.   Land-Rail.

$\frac{1}{2}$

Pl. 60

Great Bustard. (♂ & ♀)

5.

Pl. 61.

Little Bustard. &&.

Crane.

Stone-Curlew.

Macqeen's Bustard. 5.

Pl. 6.

Black-winged Pratincole.   Pratincole.
Caspian Plover.(adult&young)   Cream-coloured Courser.   2/5
        Dotterel.   Little Ringed Plover.   Ringed Plover.
                                    Kentish Plover.

Pl. 63.

Sociable Plover. (adult & young)   Killdeer Plover.

Golden Plover. (summer & winter).   Asiatic Golden Plover.

Grey Plover. (summer & winter).   Lapwing.

Grey Phalarope. (winter & summer).   Oyster catcher. (summer & winter).
Turnstone. (summer & winter).   Avocet.
Black winged Stilt.   Red-necked Phalarope.

Pl. 65.

Common Snipe.

Jack Snipe.

Woodcock.

Great Snipe.

Broad-billed Sandpiper. Terek Sandpiper. Pectoral Sandpiper. Baird's Sandpiper.

2
5

Pl. 66

Sanderling (winter & summer).
Bonaparte's Sandpiper.
Dunlin. (winter & summer.)
Knot. (winter & summer).
Little Stint (summer & autumn).
Temminck's Stint.
Purple Sandpiper (winter & summer).
American Stint.
Curlew-Sandpiper (summer & autumn).

2/5

Pl. 67.

Common Sandpiper.   Spotted Sandpiper.
                                                    Wood-Sandpiper.
        Buff-Breasted Sandpiper.   Bartram's Sandpiper.   2
Semi-palmated Sandpiper.   5
              Ruff (Varieties) & Reeve.

Pl. 68

Green Sandpiper.   Spotted Redshank. (Summer & winter).

Redshank.

Greenshank.   Red-breasted Snipe.   Marsh Sandpiper.   2

Solitary Sandpiper.   Greater Yellowshank.   5

Pl. 69.

Bar-tailed Godwit. (summer & winter.)   Black-tailed Godwit. (summer & winter.)
Eskimo Curlew.   Slender-billed Curlew.
        Whimbrel.   Common Curlew.

Pl. 70.

Whiskered Tern. (adult & young).   White-winged Black Tern. (adult & you

Black Tern.

Sooty Tern.   Gull-billed Tern (adult & young).   2/7

Caspian Tern.

Pl. 71.

Roseate Tern.   Arctic Tern.

Common Tern.

Sandwich Tern.   Little Tern.

(Adults & young.)

$\frac{2}{7}$.

Pl. 72

Ross's Gull. (summer & winter).

Common Gull. (adult & young).

Mediterranean Black-headed Gull.

Little Gull (adult & young).

Sabine's Gull.

Bonaparte's Gull.

Black-headed Gull. (summer & winter).

4

Pl. 9

A. Thorburn
1915.

Herring Gull. (adult & young).

Iceland Gull.

Lesser Black-backed Gull.

Great Black-headed Gull.

¼.

Pl. 74

Kittiwake Gull (adult & young).
Great Black-backed Gull (adult & young).
Ivory Gull.   Glaucous Gull.

Pl. 75.

Richardson's Skua.
Pomatorine Skua.

Great Skua.
Long-tailed or Buffon's Skua.

¼

Pl. 76.

Black Guillemot. (summer & winter)   Puffin. (summer & winter)
Common Guillemot.   Brünnich's Guillemot.
Razorbill (summer & winter)
Great Auk.   Little Auk. (summer & winter)

Pl. 77.

Great Northern Diver (summer & winter).

Red-throated Diver. (summer & winter)   White-billed Northern Diver.

Black-throated Diver.

Pl. 78.

Black-necked or Eared Grebe.

Red-necked Grebe.   Great Crested Grebe. $\frac{1}{3}$

Slavonian or Horned Grebe. (summer & winter)   Little Grebe. (summer & winter).

Pl. 79.

Storm. Petrel.   Leach's Fork-tailed Petrel.
Frigate. Petrel.   Madeiran Fork-tailed Petrel.
Wilson's Petrel.   Sooty Shearwater.
Little Dusky Shearwater.   Great Shearwater.

Pl. 80.

A. Thorburn. 1916.

Black-browed Albatross. (scale ½)   Manx Shearwater.   Capped Petrel.
                                         Collared Petrel.

Fulmar.   Bulwer's Petrel.   ⅓
                                         Schlegel's Petrel.

Pl. 80.

Marsh-Titmouse.

Greenland Redpoll.   Willow-Titmouse.

Greater Redpoll.   Irish Coal-Titmouse.

Hebridean Song-Thrush.   St. Kilda Wren.

2/3

Pl. 80.

Oliraceous Warbler.   Rüppell's Warbler.

Moustached Warbler.   Pied Wheatear.

Pine-Bunting.   Yellowshank.   Scottish Crossbill

2/3

NOTES ON THE PLATES

─── PLATE 1 ───

Mistle Thrush (Mistle-Thrush)
Turdus viscivorus. 26-28cm.
DISTRIBUTION: Western and central Palearctic region. Sedentary and partially migratory; northern and eastern populations moving south to winter. HABITAT: Woods, parks, gardens, conifers, upland scrub. Winters in fields and moors. FOOD: Invertebrates, and in autumn and winter, berries. STATUS: RB and MB; PV and WV.

Song Thrush (Song-Thrush)
Turdus philomelos (Turdus musicus). 22-24cm.
DISTRIBUTION: Western and central Palearctic region. Resident and migratory, northern populations moving south to winter. HABITAT: Woods and forests with ample undergrowth, scrub, and, especially in western Europe, town parks, gardens, orchards. FOOD: Invertebrates, especially snails and worms; also plant material, mainly fruits, from late summer to winter. Status: RB and MB; PV and WV. Major decline over last 20 years. ***UK Red Listed****.*

Redwing
Turdus iliacus. 21cm.
DISTRIBUTION: Northern Eurasia. Migrates south to winter. HABITAT: Forests, especially birch, alder and conifers, and scrub areas with scattered trees; in winter in farmlands, gardens and open country. FOOD: Invertebrates in autumn, also berries in winter. STATUS: Small numbers RB or MB; regular PV and WV.

Fieldfare
Turdus pilaris. 25.5cm.
DISTRIBUTION: Northern Eurasia. Resident and migratory, wintering well south. HABITAT: Forests, woodlands, often near marshes, towns. FOOD: invertebrates, also fruits late summer to early winter. STATUS: Rare but regular CB; PV and WV.

Black-throated Thrush
Turdus ruficollis (Turdus atrigularis),
Thorburn illustrated the western subspecies *T.r.atrogularis.* 23.5cm.
DISTRIBUTION: Central Asia. Winters in south Asia. HABITAT: Various forest types, open riparian woodlands and scattered subalpine scrub. FOOD: Invertebrates and in winter berries and seeds. STATUS: SV, mainly in late autumn and winter. [Dark-throated Thrush]

─── PLATE 2 ───

Dusky Thrush
Turdus naumanni (Turdus dubius),
Thorburn illustrated the northern subspecies *T.n.eunomus.* 23cm.
DISTRIBUTION: Breeds central and south-east Siberia. Winters in south Asia and Japan. HABITAT: Open forests, woodland edges, scrub. FOOD: Invertebrates, especially insects and snails, also berries and seeds. STATUS: SV, mainly in autumn and winter.

White's Thrush
Zoothera dauma (Turdus varius). 27cm.
DISTRIBUTION: Locally in eastern Eurasia. Northern populations winter to India, south-eastern Asia and northern Philippines. HABITAT: Coniferous and deciduous forests, woodlands, undergrowth. FOOD: Insects, worms, and berries. STATUS: SV in autumn and winter. [Scaly Thrush]

Siberian Thrush
Zoothera sibirica (Turdus sibiricus). 22cm.
DISTRIBUTION: Eastern Asia. Winters to south-east Asia. HABITAT: Forest undergrowth. FOOD: Chiefly insects and worms, also fruits and berries. STATUS: SV in winter.

Blackbird
Turdus merula. 24-25cm.
DISTRIBUTION: Western and southern Palearctic. Resident though northern populations move south or west to winter in southern or western Europe. HABITAT: Wide variety, including woodlands, farmlands, heaths, upland moors, and towns. FOOD: Mainly insects and earthworms; also fruit from late summer to early winter. STATUS: RB and MB; PV and WV. Common and widespread.[Common Blackbird]

Ring Ouzel (Ring-Ouzel)
Turdus torquatus. 23-24cm.
DISTRIBUTION: West and southwest Palearctic. HABITAT: Open moorland and hills with rocky outcrops and sparse trees, and in conifer woodlands. Winters mainly in north-west Africa. FOOD: In spring and early summer chiefly insects and earthworms; at other times, mainly fruit. STATUS: MB and PV; SV.

Rock Thrush (Rock-Thrush)
Monticola saxatilis. 18.5cm.
DISTRIBUTION: Southern Palearctic. Most winter in Afrotropics. HABITAT: Open rocky hills often with scattered trees or shrubs, in Africa in savanna, erosion areas, gardens, rocky moorlands and around buildings. FOOD: Mostly large insects. STATUS: SV, most in April to June. [Rufous-tailed Rock-Thrush]

─── PLATE 3 ───

Wheatear
Oenanthe oenanthe (Saxicola oenanthe). 14.5-15.5cm.
DISTRIBUTION: Palearctic, northern North America, north-western Africa. Winters central Africa. HABITAT: Stony barrens, tundra, plains, deserts, pastures, sea-coasts. FOOD: Invertebrates, chiefly insects, also berries. STATUS: MB and PV; marked decrease in southern England. [Northern Wheatear]

Isabelline Wheatear
Oenanthe isabellina (Saxicola isabellina). 16.5cm.
DISTRIBUTION: South and central Eurasia. Winters in north-east Africa and from Arabia east to central India. HABITAT: Plains, stony deserts. FOOD: Chiefly invertebrates. STATUS: SV.

Black-eared Wheatear (Black-throated Wheatear)
Oenanthe hispanica (Saxicola occidentalis).
Thorburn illustrated a male black-throated morph of the western Mediterranean subspecies *Oenanthe hispanica hispanica.* 14.5cm.
DISTRIBUTION: Southern Palearctic. Wintering in northern tropical Africa. HABITAT: Open rocky areas, barren or with sparse trees and shrubs, open farmlands. FOOD: Almost entirely insects. STATUS: SV.

Thorburn also illustrated a male pale-throated morph of the eastern Mediterranean and Middle East subspecies of the **Black-eared Wheatear** *Oenanthe hispanica melanoleuca,* for which he used the scientific name *Saxicola stapazina*. This subspecies has also been recorded as a scarce visitor.

Desert Wheater
Oenanthe deserti (Saxicola deserti). 14-15cm.
DISTRIBUTION: South-western, southern and central Palearctic. Winters from north and northeastern Africa and Arabia east to India. HABITAT: Varying habitats over extensive range; penetrates litte beyond desert fringe. FOOD: Chiefly insects. STATUS: SV, mainly in autumn and spring.

Pied Wheatear (Eastern Pied Wheatear)
Oenanthe pleschanka. 14.5cm.
DISTRIBUTION: South-central Eurasia. Winters eastern Africa and north-eastwards to south-west Arabia. HABITAT: Stony ground with sparse vegetation, deserts, river banks, farmlands and in winter also human

settlements. Food: Almost entirely insects, sometimes also berries. Status: SV, mainly in autumn.

Black Wheatear
Oenanthe leucura (Saxicola leucura), from south-west Europe and north-west Africa, was deleted from the official British and Irish List in 1993 (Ibis 135: 493-499).

Stonechat
Saxicola torquata (Pratincola rubicola). 12.5cm.
Distribution: Palearctic and African region. Western populations resident or partially migratory, eastern populations highly migratory wintering southwards. Habitat: Diverse; open country, usually rocky with scattered bushes and trees, lowlands to mountains. Food: Invertebrates, chiefly insects. Status: Relatively common RB and MB; SV. [Common Stonechat]

Thorburn also illustrated the central and eastern Eurasian subspecies *S.t.maura,* the **Siberian Stonechat**, which he called the **Eastern Stonechat**. This subspecies, and the subspecies *S.t.variegata,* have been identified as SVs.

— PLATE 4 —

Whinchat
Saxicola rubetra (Pratincola rubetra). 12.5cm.
Distribution: Western Palearctic. Winters mainly in tropical Africa. Habitat: Heaths, scrub and grasslands with bushes, meadows and marshes. Food: Invertebrates, chiefly insects, also some seeds and berries. Status: MB and PV.

Redstart
Phoenicurus phoenicurus (Ruticilla phoenicurus). 14cm.
Distribution: Palearctic. Winters in the African Sahel zone and south-west Arabia. Habitat: Fairly open, deciduous and coniferous forests and woods, parkland, gardens, and farmlands. Food: Invertebrates, chiefly insects, spiders, and some fruits. Status: MB and PV; SV. [Common Redstart]

Black Redstart
Phoenicurus ochruros (Ruticilla titys). 14.5cm.
Distribution: Palearctic. Resident, partial migrant or migrant wintering from west Europe and Mediterranean region south to north and north-east Africa and east across south Asia to south India, Burma and north Indochina. Habitat: Rocky, stony, boulder strewn terrain, cliffs, and buildings; has evolved close commensalism with man. Food: Mainly invertebrates and fruit. Status: Small population of MB and RB, also some PV and WV; SV.

Bluethroat (Arctic Bluethroat)
Luscinia svecica (Cyanecula suecica). 14cm.
Distribution: Eurasia. Mainly migratory, wintering Mediterranean south to northern Afrotropics and east to Indian subcontinent and south-east Asia. Habitat: Bushes, undergrowth, scrub, wooded tundra and shrubby wetlands, swamps. Food: Chiefly terrestrial invertebrates, mainly insects; in autumn also seeds and fruits. Status: CB(1968), regular and annual PV.

Thorburn's **White-spotted Bluethroat** *(Cyanecula leucocyana)* is the white-spotted subspecies *L.svecica cyanecula:* both the south European L.s.cyanecula and the Scandinavian red-spotted subspecies *L.s.svecica* have occurred in Britain, the latter more commonly.

Robin (Redbreast)
Erithacus rubecula. 14cm.
Distribution: Upper and middle latitudes of west Palearctic. Winters from British Isles south to north Africa and south-east through Europe. Habitat: Essentially a bird of dense vegetation; shrubs, woodlands, forests, towns. British race 'tame' but continental races noticeably wilder. Food: Invertebrates, especially insects; also fruit and seeds in winter. Status: Common and widespread, RB and MB; PV and WV. [European Robin]

Nightingale
Luscinia megarhynchos (Daulias luscinia). 16.5cm.
Distribution: West Palearctic in middle and lower-middle latitudes. Winters in tropical Africa. Habitat: Varies from thickets or woods near water, orchards, shrubbery to drier areas such as bushy coastal sand-dunes and maquis. Food: Terrestrial invertebrates, also berries in late summer. Status: MB and PV, range and numbers have decreased; also SV. [Common Nightingale]

— PLATE 5 —

Thrush Nightingale
Luscinia luscinia (Daulias philomela). 16.5cm.
Distribution: Northern Eurasia. Winters in east and south-east Africa. Habitat: Dense, damp thickets, often by river banks or near standing water with ground cover. Food: Invertebrates and some fruit. Status: Increasingly regular SV.

Whitethroat
Sylvia communis (Sylvia cinerea) 14cm.
Distribution: Palearctic. Winters widely in Africa, especially in the Sahel and other semi-arid regions further south and east. Habitat: Typically open cover, consisting variously of tall herbage, bushes, thickets, field margins, woodland and swamp edges. Food: During breeding season mainly insects; in winter berries predominate. Status: MB and PV, with large but fluctuating numbers. [Greater or Common Whitethroat]

Lesser Whitethroat
Sylvia curruca. 12.5-13.5cm.
Distribution: Palearctic. Winters from tropical eastern Africa east to India. Habitat: Varied; prefers well spaced, tall bushes, shrubs, hedges, plantations, gardens, parks; in winter in thorny bushes, savanna, palm groves, scrub jungle with undergrowth. Food: Chiefly insects, also berries in late summer and autumn. Status: MB and PV, with fluctuating numbers; SV.

Orphean Warbler
Sylvia hortensis (Sylvia orphea). 15cm.
Distribution: Patchy breeding range in southern Europe, north-western Africa, Asia Minor, Transcaucasia, and south-central Asia. Winters in Sahel zone south of the Sahara, Arabia and India. Habitat: Open woodlands, orchards, olive groves and gardens; in winter in open bush and Acacia scrub. Food: Chiefly invertebrates, also berries. Status: SV.

Sardinian Warbler
Sylvia melanocephala. 13.5cm.
Distribution: Mediterranean zone. Sedentary and partially migratory, mainly to north-western and north-eastern Africa. Habitat: Low scrub (maquis) tall undergrowth, and areas with close-growing trees. Food: Chiefly insects, also fruits in autumn and winter. Status: SV.

Blackcap
Sylvia atricapilla. 13cm.
Distribution: Western Palearctic. Sedentary to migratory with widely dispersed wintering grounds in the Mediterranean and Africa, both north and south of the Sahara. Habitat: Mainly in mature deciduous woodlands with shrubby undergrowth, plantations, parks, gardens; in winter also in savanna, Acacia steppes, mangrove scrubs. Food: Chiefly insects in breeding season; mainly berries at other times. Status: MB (increasing), PV and some WV.

Garden Warbler
Sylvia borin (Sylvia hortensis). 14cm.
DISTRIBUTION: Western Palearctic. Winters in Africa south of the Sahara. HABITAT: Mainly deciduous woodland edges with dense shrub or scrub layers; in winter also forests, bush, savanna, gardens. FOOD: Chiefly insects in breeding season; mainly berries at other times. STATUS: MB and PV.

Barred Warbler
Sylvia nisoria. 15.5cm.
DISTRIBUTION: Central Eurasia. Winters eastern Africa south of the Sahara. HABITAT: Typically in stratified habitat of herb layer and bushes (often thorny), interspersed with taller trees; in winter, typically along dry river beds in dense thickets. FOOD: Chiefly insects, also berries in late summer and autumn. STATUS: Scarce PV, mainly autumn.

—————— PLATE 6 ——————

Subalpine Warbler
Sylvia cantillans (Sylvia subalpina). 12cm.
DISTRIBUTION: South-western Palearctic. Winters on the southern edge of the Sahara. HABITAT: Mainly on dry slopes with dense scrub, also open woodlands with scattered bushes. FOOD: Chiefly adult and larval insects. STATUS: Regular SV.

Dartford Warbler
Sylvia undata. 12.5cm.
DISTRIBUTION: South-western Europe and north-western Africa. Mainly resident; some European birds move south to winter as far as north-western Africa. HABITAT: Dense thorny bushes and lowland heaths. Outside breeding season also in open agriculture plains with some scrub. FOOD: Invertebrates, especially insects and in winter, spiders, also fruits in autumn and winter in continental Europe. STATUS: RB small population southern England. **UK Red Listed**.

Yellow-browed Warbler
Phylloscopus inornatus (Phylloscopus superciliosus). 10cm.
DISTRIBUTION: Eastern and south-central Eurasia. Winters from Near East, Egypt east to India and to south-eastern Asia. HABITAT: Open growth of mainly deciduous trees and shrubs, often in riverain forest. FOOD: Invertebrates, chiefly insects. STATUS: Regular and increasing autumn PV. [Inornate Warbler]

Pallas's Warbler (Pallas's Willow-Warbler)
Phylloscopus prolegus. 9cm.
DISTRIBUTION: Eastern Asia. Winters in southern China, India and Indochina. HABITAT: Taiga-type coniferous forest with thick undergrowth, open woodlands with shrubby meadows. On passage common in riverain woodlands. FOOD: Little information; include adult and larval insects. STATUS: Scarce but regular PV in autumn.
[Lemon-rumped Warbler or Pallas's Leaf Warbler]

Greenish Warbler (Greenish Willow-Warbler)
Phylloscopus trochiloides (Phylloscopus viridanus). 10cm.
DISTRIBUTION: Eurasia. Winters India to south-eastern Asia. HABITAT: Fringes and clearings of forests, also copses, parks and thickets. In winter also in cultivated country, orchards and gardens. FOOD: Mostly invertebrates, especially insects. STATUS: SV.

Chiffchaff
Phylloscopus collybita (Phylloscopus rufus). 10-11cm.
DISTRIBUTION: Eurasia. Mostly migratory, within or south of breeding areas; winters south to northern Afrotropics, Middle East, Pakistan and northern India. HABITAT: Open woodlands with undergrowth, on passage and in winter quarters also in scrub, reeds, gardens. FOOD: Chiefly small insects and larvae. STATUS: Common MB, PV and small number WV. [Eurasian or Common Chiffchaff]

Willow Warbler (Willow-Wren)
Phylloscopus trochilus. 10.5-11.5cm.
DISTRIBUTION: Eurasia. Winters in sub-Saharan Africa. HABITAT: Woods, particularly along edges and in clearings, bushes, young conifer plantations, hedges and gardens. In winter in areas with trees, bushes and grass. FOOD: Insects and spiders; in autumn also berries. Status: Common MB and PV.

Wood Warbler (Wood-Wren)
Phylloscopus sibilatrix. 12cm.
DISTRIBUTION: Western and central Eurasia. Winters in sub-Saharan Africa from Sierra Leone east to Uganda. HABITAT: Deciduous, mixed and coniferous forests, typically with closed canopy and of different ages. Winters mainly in open forests and wooded savanna. FOOD: Invertebrates, especially insects; also fruit and seeds in autumn. STATUS: Common MB and scarce PV.

—————— PLATE 7 ——————

Rufous Bush Chat (Rufous Warbler)
Cercotrichas galactotes (Aðdon galactodes). 15cm.
DISTRIBUTION: Southern Palearctic, south-central Eurasia, sub-Saharan Africa. Eurasian and North African populations migratory, wintering in nouthern Afrotropics; sub-Saharan breeding populations are resident. HABITAT: Dry scrub, acacia thickets, hedges, orchards, towns. In Africa, winter particularly, in dry Acacia scrub. FOOD: Mainly insects and earthworms; occasionally fruit. STATUS: SV. [Rufous-tailed Scrub-Robin]

Radde's Warbler (Radde's Bush-Warbler)
Phylloscopus schwarzi (Lusciniola schwarzi). 12.5cm.
DISTRIBUTION: Eastern Asia. Winters in south-eastern Asia. HABITAT: Taiga, forest steppe, bushes, forest edges. In winter mainly in bushes and tall grass. FOOD: Chiefly insects. STATUS: SV in autumn.

Icterine Warbler
Hippolais icterina (Hypolais icterina). 13.5cm.
DISTRIBUTION: Eurasia. Winters in sub-Saharan Africa, chiefly south of the equator. HABITAT: Open and edge woodlands with rich undergrowth, also orchards, parks and gardens. In winter quarters frequents thornveld. FOOD: Chiefly insects; also fruits late summer. STATUS: CB (possibly bred late 19th century, 1907 and 1970) and annual, scarce, mainly autumn PV.

Melodious Warbler
Hippolais polyglotta (Hypolais polyglotta). 13cm.
DISTRIBUTION: Palearctic, in south-western Europe, and north-western Africa. Winters in West Africa north of the equator. HABITAT: Woodlands and shrub thickets, often near water. In winter in savanna, mangroves, forest clearings and dense bushes. FOOD: Chiefly insects; also fruit before migration. STATUS: Scarce, annual, mostly autumn PV.

Reed Warbler (Reed-Warbler)
Acrocephalus scirpaceus (Acrocephalus streperus). 13cm.
DISTRIBUTION: Western and central Palearctic. Winters in tropical Africa. HABITAT: Largely confined to reedbeds, often feeding in adjacent woodlands and arable fields and in willows by water. In winter in swamp vegetation, thickets, tall grass. FOOD: Chiefly insects and spiders; berries in autumn. STATUS: Common MB, and PV. [Eurasian Reed-Warbler]

Marsh Warbler (Marsh-Warbler)
Acrocephalus palustris. 13cm.
DISTRIBUTION: Western Eurasia. Winters in eastern and south-eastern Africa. HABITAT: Typically in tall dense vegetation by overgrown ditches, streams or marshes, also disused farmlands, standing cereals. In winter essentially arboreal. FOOD: Chiefly insects and arachnids, some snails and also berries in autumn. STATUS: MB, scarce and local, 11-13 pairs (1989-93); also scarce PV. **UK Red Listed**.

—————————— PLATE 8 ——————————

Great Reed Warbler (Great Reed-Warbler)
Acrocephalus arundinaceus (Acrocephalus turdoides). 19-20cm.
DISTRIBUTION: Eurasia. Winters south of the Sahara and in southern Asia, East Indies and Philippines. HABITAT: Mainly aquatic emergent vegetation, especially reedbeds. In African winter quarters in swamp vegetation and varied cover, often not near water. FOOD: Chiefly insects, some fruit outside breeding season. STATUS: SV. [Great Reed-Warbler]

Sedge Warbler (Sedge-Warbler)
Acrocephalus schoenobaenus (Acrocephalus phragmitis). 13cm.
DISTRIBUTION: Eurasia. Winters widely in Africa south of the Sahara. HABITAT: Tangled undergrowth mainly by water, including drier reedbed margins with shrubs, overgrown ditches, and cover away from water. In winter uses a wide variety of freshwater habitats. FOOD: Chiefly insects, also some plant material outside breeding season. STATUS: Common MB and PV.

Aquatic Warbler
Acrocephalus paludicola (Acrocephalus aquaticus). 13cm.
DISTRIBUTION: Western Palearctic. Winters in West Africa south of the Sahara. HABITAT: Lowland freshwater and brackish marshes, fen mires in river valleys, partially drained hay meadows, boggy grasslands. Outside the breeding season, similar habitat. FOOD: Chiefly insects and spiders. STATUS: Rare, annual, autumn PV. **UK Red Listed** and of **Global Conservation Concern**.

Grasshopper Warbler (Grasshopper-Warbler)
Locustrella naevia. 12.5cm.
DISTRIBUTION: Eurasia. Winters mainly in West Africa south of the Sahara and east to India. HABITAT: Rough grasslands, scrubs, fringes of marshes and other wet areas with ground cover. FOOD: Chiefly insects. STATUS: MB and PV; has declined over last 25 years. [Common Grasshopper Warbler]

Savi's Warbler
Locustella luscinioides. 14cm.
DISTRIBUTION: Locally in Eurasia. Winters mainly in eastern and southeastern tropical Africa. HABITAT: Typically in rank herbaceous vegetation by ditches or marshes and sometimes in standing cereals. FOOD: Insects. STATUS: FB and CB, 1-15 pairs (1989-93), southern and eastern England) and scarce PV.

Cetti's Warbler
Cettia cetti. 14cm.
DISTRIBUTION: Southern Eurasia. Sedentary to migratory; north-eastern populations winter south to southern Afghanistan, Pakistan and north-western India. HABITAT: Dense, tangled, low scrub near water and, especially in winter, reedbeds. FOOD: Chiefly insects and some other invertebrates. STATUS: Scarce RB in southern and eastern England; first bred 1972, now 17-282 pairs (1989-93). Scarce PV.

—————————— PLATE 9 ——————————

Goldcrest
Regulus regulus (Regulus cristatus). 9cm.
DISTRIBUTION: Locally in Palearctic. Resident to migratory; winters in southern parts of breeding range and beyond to Mediterranean region, Near and Middle East, Himalayas and central and southern China. HABITAT: Forests and woods, mainly coniferous but also mixed and deciduous. In winter also in hedges, scrub and smaller gardens. FOOD: Chiefly insects and spiders. STATUS: Common RB, PV and WV.

Firecrest
Regulus ignicapillus. 9cm.
DISTRIBUTION: Western Palearctic. Northern and eastern populations mainly migratory, wintering in western Europe and the Mediterranean region; southern populations mainly resident. HABITAT: Woodlands, coniferous, mixed and deciduous. In winter also fringe and scrub. FOOD: Invertebrates, especially springtails, spiders and aphids. STATUS: Small and fluctuating numbers; MB or RB, PV and WV.

Dunnock (Hedge Sparrow)
Prunella modularis (Accentor modularis). 14.5cm.
DISTRIBUTION: Western Eurasia. Resident, partial migrant and in northern and central Europe total migrant to Mediterranean region and northern Africa. HABITAT: Gardens and parks with good cover, wooded tundra, montane scrub and forests. FOOD: Chiefly insects, also seeds in winter. STATUS: RB, PV and WV; small but progressive decline. [Hedge Sparrow or Hedge Accentor]

Alpine Accentor
Prunella collaris (Accentor collaris). 18cm.
DISTRIBUTION: Locally in mountains of Palearctic. Sedentary with some wandering within or just south of the breeding range in winter. HABITAT: Above tree-line among alpine grasslands strewn with boulders or large stones. FOOD: Largely insects, and in late summer and winter seeds. STATUS: SV.

Dipper
Cinclus cinclus (Cinclus aquaticus). 18cm.
DISTRIBUTION: Palearctic. Mostly resident, though northern populations partial migrants. HABITAT: Typically swift-flowing, shallow, rocky streams and rivers, usually of mountainous and hilly regions. FOOD: Chiefly aquatic invertebrates, especially caddis-flies. STATUS: RB and SV. [White-throated Dipper]

Nuthatch
Sitta europaea (Sitta caesia). 14cm.
DISTRIBUTION: Palearctic, south-central and eastern China. Essentially sedentary. HABITAT: Trees, mainly deciduous, in woodlands, parks, gardens, hedgerows. FOOD: Chiefly insects and spiders; also seeds in autumn and winter. STATUS: RB. Longterm gradual increase. [Wood Nuthatch]

Wren
Troglodytes troglodytes (Troglodytes parulus). 9-10cm.
DISTRIBUTION: Palearctic and North America. Northernmost continental, and montane populations, are partially migratory, or migratory, wintering within or south of breeding range. HABITAT: In low cover in wide range of habitats, especially damp deciduous or mixed woods with thick undergrowth, overgrown valleys with streams, untended garden-woodland areas. FOOD: Chiefly insects and spiders. STATUS: RB and some WV and PV from European continent. Common; numbers fluctuate according to winter weather. [Winter Wren]

—————————— PLATE 10 ——————————

Bearded Tit (Bearded Titmouse)
Panurus biarmicus. 12.5cm.
DISTRIBUTION: Locally in Palearctic. Mainly sedentary, with some dispersal within or just south of breeding range. HABITAT: In large reedbeds and associated, dense, tall, non-woody vegetation. FOOD: Chiefly insects in summer; mainly seeds in late autumn and winter. STATUS: RB (Eastern England), WV and PV. [Bearded Parrotbill, but affinities uncertain]

Long-tailed Tit (Long-tailed Titmouse)
Aegithalos caudatus (Acredula caudata). 14cm.
DISTRIBUTION: Palearctic. Northern populations are irregularly migratory, reaching southern parts of the breeding range in winter. HABITAT: Thick hedges, scrub, bushy heaths, also in winter deciduous woodlands. FOOD: Chiefly insects; occasionally seeds in autumn and winter. STATUS: RB, numbers much reduced by hard winters; SV.

Great Tit (Great Titmouse)
Parus major. 14cm.
DISTRIBUTION: Palearctic, eastern and southern Asia. Resident; northern populations irregularly have eruptive movements to the south. HABITAT: Deciduous and mixed woodlands with undergrowth, also where trees or shrubs present, e.g., towns, farms, and mangroves and bamboo stands. FOOD: Mainly insects, especially lepidopteran caterpillars and beetles, also spiders; seeds and fruits important in winter. STATUS: Common RB, mainly sedentary; WV, immigrants from the Continent.

Coal Tit (Coal Titmouse)
Parus ater. 11.5cm.
DISTRIBUTION: Palearctic: Northern populations are partially migratory, some birds reaching southern parts of the breeding range and beyond. HABITAT: Coniferous, mixed and deciduous woodlands, scrub, gardens. FOOD: Chiefly insects and spiders; also seeds. STATUS: Common RB, PV in small numbers from the Continent.

Marsh Tit (Marsh Titmouse)
Parus palustris. 11.5cm.
DISTRIBUTION: Eurasia. Mainly sedentary. HABITAT: Mixed deciduous woodlands, copses, parks, gardens with trees. FOOD: Chiefly insects and spiders in breeding season; also, at other times, seeds, nuts, and berries. STATUS: RB, small long-term decline.

Blue Tit (Blue Titmouse)
Parus caeruleus. 11.5cm.
DISTRIBUTION: Western Palearctic. Resident, though in centre and north of range irregular eruptive migration to west and south. HABITAT: Arboreal, occurs in most areas with trees, though avoids conifers; outside breeding season also in scrub, bushy thickets, reedbeds. FOOD: Chiefly insects and spiders; also seeds and fruits outside breeding season. STATUS: Common RB; WV in small numbers from the Continent.

Crested Tit (Crested Titmouse)
Parus cristatus. 11.5cm.
DISTRIBUTION: Europe, except extreme north and south-east. Mainly sedentary. HABITAT: Mature pine forests and mixed woodlands. FOOD: Chiefly insects and spiders; outside the breeding season also conifer seeds. STATUS: RB in Scotland; SV, few records of Continental vagrants.

─────────── PLATE 11 ───────────

Treecreeper (Tree-creeper)
Certhia familiaris. 12.5cm.
DISTRIBUTION: Eurasia. Sedentary to partial migrant. HABITAT: Arboreal, in deciduous, mixed and coniferous woodlands, parks and gardens with trees. FOOD: Chiefly insects and spiders, also some seeds in winter. STATUS: RB and occasional SV from Continent. [Eurasian Tree-creeper]

Wallcreeper (Wall-creeper)
Tichodroma muraria. 16.5cm.
DISTRIBUTION: Southern Palearctic. Short or longer distance migrant and some sedentary. HABITAT: Cliffs, rocks, stone buildings. FOOD: Small insects and spiders. STATUS: Irregular SV.

Pied or White Wagtail
Motacilla alba (Motacilla lugubris). 18cm.
DISTRIBUTION: Palearctic and western Alaska. Mainly migratory, wintering in southern parts of breeding range and south to Mediterranean area, tropics and subtropics of Africa, India and south-east Asia. HABITAT: Open country, tundra to desert edges, shores, parks, farmlands, often near water. FOOD: Small invertebrates, chiefly adult and larval insects, and some seeds. STATUS: MB and RB the British race, M.a.yarrelli, some decline noted. CB and PV M.a.alba.

Thorburn's illustration of the **White Wagtail** shows the race *M.a.alba*, which occurs in Britain as a regular passage migrant (PV) and rare breeder (CB).

Grey Wagtail
Motacilla cinerea (Motacilla melanope). 18-19cm.
DISTRIBUTION: Palearctic. Partially migratory or migratory, wintering in southern parts of the breeding range and beyond to Africa as far south as Malawi, Middle East, India, south-east Asia and New Guinea. HABITAT: Fast-flowing streams and rivers; in winter also by lowland, slower-flowing waters, lakes and coastal marshes. FOOD: Chiefly adult and larval insects. STATUS: RB and PV from the Continent.

Yellow Wagtail (Blue-headed Wagtail)
Motacilla flava. 17cm.
DISTRIBUTION: Palearctic and Alaska. Most populations migratory, wintering mainly in Afrotropics, India, and south-east Asia. HABITAT: Open damp meadows, marshes, river banks, lake margins, bogs; outside breeding season more widespread. FOOD: Small invertebrates, mainly adult and larval insects.

Thorburn has illustrated three races of the **Yellow Wagtail:**

Yellow Wagtail
M.f.flavissima, which he names *M.raii*. Breeds in Britain and locally on continental coast of north-west Europe. STATUS: Fairly common MB and PV, though decline noted.

Grey-headed Wagtail
M.f.thunbergi, which he names *M.viridis*. Breeds in Fenno-Scandia and Russia east to northwestern Siberia. STATUS: PV.

Blue-headed Wagtail
M.f.flava, which he names *M.flava*. Breeds in southernmost Fenno-Scandia to the Urals, south to France, northern Italy and Rumania. STATUS: CB and PV.

─────────── PLATE 12 ───────────

Tree Pipit (Tree-pipit)
Anthus trivialis. 15cm.
DISTRIBUTION: Eurasia. Winters from Mediterranean region east to Indian subcontinent and south to Afrotropics. HABITAT: In breeding season and winter quarters in areas of trees and open ground, such as open woodlands, heath/scrub with scattered trees, forest margins. FOOD: Chiefly insects; also some plant material in winter. STATUS: MB and PV.

Meadow Pipit (Meadow-pipit)
Anthus pratensis. 14.5cm.
DISTRIBUTION: North-western Palearctic. Resident or partial migrant in west of its range and wholly migratory in the north and east, wintering in southern parts of breeding range and further south to Mediterranean region and the Middle East. HABITAT: Open, thinly vegetated ground such as moors, pastures, montane meadows, coastal dunes. FOOD: Mainly invertebrates; some seeds in autumn and winter. STATUS: MB, RB, PV and WV. Stable.

Red-throated Pipit
Anthus cervinus. 15cm.
DISTRIBUTION: Northern Palearctic and western Alaska. Winters mainly in tropics of Africa and south-east Asia. HABITAT: Shrubby or mossy tundra and swamps of willow and birch. Winters on irrigated ground with short grass and shallow water, lake mudflats, moorlands. FOOD: Chiefly insects, also aquatic snails and some seeds. STATUS: SV in the autumn.

Tawny Pipit
Anthus campestris. 16.5cm.
DISTRIBUTION: Western and central Palearctic. Winters in Sahel zone of south Sahara and Arabia, southern Afghanistan and India. HABITAT: Typically open, dry areas with sparse and broken vegetation cover, bare sandy patches and perches for singing. In winter in coastal zones, barest parts of thorn-savanna and edge of deserts. FOOD: Chiefly insects, also, and mainly in winter, seeds. STATUS: Regular PV.

Richard's Pipit
Anthus richardi. 18cm.
DISTRIBUTION: Eastern and central Asia. Winters in southern Asia from India to southern China and south-eastern Asia. HABITAT: Chiefly open grasslands. FOOD: Mainly invertebrates, especially insects, and some seeds. STATUS: Regular PV, mainly in autumn.

Water Pipit (Alpine or Water-Pipit)
Anthus spinoletta (Anthus spipoletta). 16.5-17cm.
DISTRIBUTION: Palearctic. Dispersive and migratory, wintering mainly south to northern Africa and Middle East. HABITAT: Locally in mountains on grassy slopes, moist meadows, watercourses or snowmelt. FOOD: Mainly invertebrates and some plant material. STATUS: Regular PV and WV, in small numbers.

Rock Pipit
Anthus petrosus (Anthus obscurus). 16.5-17cm.
DISTRIBUTION: Western Palearctic. Resident and migratory, wintering from British Isles to eastern Mediterranean region. HABITAT: On rocky sea-cliffs and crags; also outside breeding season on other coastal sites and saltmarshes. FOOD: Chiefly invertebrates, also some seeds. STATUS: RB. Scandinavian race regular PV and WV.

———————————— PLATE 13 ————————————

Great Grey Shrike
Lanius excubitor. 24-25cm.
DISTRIBUTION: Palearctic and northern Northern America. Winters within, or just south of, the breeding range. HABITAT: Typically in semi-open country with scattered trees, bushes and short grasslands. FOOD: Chiefly insects (mainly beetles), small mammals and on occasions, birds and reptiles. STATUS: Regular but declining PV and WV. [Northern Shrike]

Lesser Grey Shrike
Lanius minor. 20cm.
DISTRIBUTION: Central Palearctic. Winters in southern Africa. HABITAT: In open lowlands and hills, especially in orchards, groves, parks, woodland edges and overgrown ditches. In winter favours arid Acacia country, extending into deserts. FOOD: Insects, particularly beetles, and occasionally grasshoppers. STATUS: In most years SV.

Red-backed Shrike
Lanius collurio. 17cm.
DISTRIBUTION: Palearctic. Winters in eastern tropical and southern Africa. HABITAT: Open, meadow areas with scattered bushes, hedgerows, forest clearings and edges, scrub, farmlands, heaths. In winter in open thorny or bushy country. FOOD: Chiefly insects; also small rodents, birds, lizards. STATUS: Now very rare CB and regular but scarce PV. *UK Red Listed.*

Woodchat Shrike
Lanius senator (Lanius pomeranus). 18cm.
DISTRIBUTION: South-western Palearctic. Winters mainly south of the Sahara but north of the equator. HABITAT: Typically in areas with trees or shrubs interspersed with clearings of short vegetation, such as grazed scrubland, woodlands or orchards. In winter, mainly Acacia savanna and patches of cultivation. FOOD: Chiefly invertebrates,

mainly insects; occasionally small vertebrates. STATUS: Scarce but regular PV.

Masked Shrike
Lanius nubicus, from south-central Asia. Thorburn included this species on the basis of specimen obtained in Kent in July 1905. This specimen was among the 'Hastings Rarities' and is no longer accepted in the British-Irish List.

———————————— PLATE 14 ————————————

Golden Oriole
Oriolus oriolus (Oriolus galbula). 24cm.
DISTRIBUTION: Palearctic. Winters Africa south of the Sahara and in the Indian region. HABITAT: Deciduous woodlands. parks, gardens. FOOD: Insects and in late summer, autumn and winter, berries. STATUS: Rare but now regular MB in East Anglia, also regular PV, mainly in the spring. [Eurasian Golden-Oriole]

Waxwing
Bombycilla garrulus (Ampelus garrulus). 18cm.
DISTRIBUTION: Northern Eurasia and north-western North America. Partial migrant, often making eruptive southern and south-western movements, within and beyond the breeding range. HABITAT: In coniferous and mixed forests; outside breeding season also in fruit-bearing tree and shrub sites, such as parks, gardens, hedgerows. FOOD: In summer mainly insects; in winter, chiefly fruit, also buds and flowers. STATUS: Irregular WV. [Bohemian Waxwing]

Spotted Flycatcher
Muscicapa striata (Muscicapa grisola). 14.5cm.
DISTRIBUTION: Palearctic. Winters in sub-Saharan Africa. HABITAT: Open woodlands, especially in clearings and along edges, also parks and gardens with trees, orchards. Similar in winter quarters. FOOD: Chiefly insects, especially Diptera and Hymenoptera; in autumn also berries. STATUS: MB and PV: considerable decline in breeding population in last 25 years and now *UK Red Listed.*

Asian Brown Flycatcher
Muscicapa daurica (Muscicapa latirostris), from southern and eastern Asia, was included by Thorburn on the basis of a specimen shot May 21st, 1909, near Lydd in Kent. This record, a 'Hastings Rarity', was rejected in 1963. The species was reinstated in 1994, though because of the possibility of a captive escape, was retained in category (D1) pending further information on patterns of natural vagrancy and the situation in captivity.

Pied Flycatcher
Ficedula hypoleuca (Muscicapa atricapilla). 13cm.
DISTRIBUTION: Western and central Palearctic. Winters in West Africa, south of the Sahara and mainly north of the Gulf of Guinea. HABITAT: Chiefly mature open deciduous and mixed woodlands, wooded parklands and gardens, orchards, towns. In winter in forests, woodlands, savanna, gardens. FOOD: Mainly insects; fruit and seeds in small amounts in late summer and on migration. STATUS: MB and PV. [European Pied Flycatcher]

Collared Flycatcher
Ficedula albicollis (Muscicapa collaris). 13cm.
DISTRIBUTION: Central and south-eastern Europe. Winters in Africa mainly south of the equator. HABITAT: Open forests, woodlands, wooded parklands, gardens, orchards. FOOD: Arthropods, chiefly insects. STATUS: Irregular SV.

Red-breasted Flycatcher
Ficedula parva (Muscicapa parva). 11.5cm.
DISTRIBUTION: Eurasia. Winters mainly in Pakistan, India and south-eastern

Asia. HABITAT: Mixed and deciduous forests with much undergrowth near water and clearings, also orchards, vineyards and spruce forests. In winter in forest plantations, groves, orchards and gardens. FOOD: Chiefly insects and other invertebrates. STATUS: Scarce but regular PV.

——————— PLATE 15 ———————

Swallow
Hirundo rustica. 17-19cm.
DISTRIBUTION: Palearctic and Nearctic. Winters south to southern Africa, East Indies, northern Australia, Philippines and Micronesia; and from Middle America and West Indies south to southern South America. HABITAT: Open country, usually near water, farmlands, towns. FOOD: Chiefly airborne insects. STATUS: MB and PV; declined since 1980. [Barn Swallow]

Red-rumped Swallow
Hirundo daurica (Hirundo rufula). 16-17cm.
DISTRIBUTION: Southern Palearctic, western and eastern Africa, southern and eastern Asia. Northern populations migratory; winter range unclear, but mainly south from southern Eurasia to Indian subregion, southern China and Indochina, and to tropical Africa. HABITAT: Open, hilly country, river gorges and valleys, also cultivated areas and human habitation. FOOD: Chiefly airborne insects. STATUS: Regular SV.

House Martin (Martin)
Delichon urbica (Chelidon urbica). 12.5cm.
DISTRIBUTION: Palearctic. Winters in Africa south of the Sahara, Assam to Indochina, southern and south-eastern Asia. HABITAT: Open and semi-open country, urban areas. FOOD: Chiefly airborne insects. STATUS: MB and PV. [Northern House Martin]

Sand Martin (Sand-Martin)
Riparia riparia (Cotile riparia). 12cm.
DISTRIBUTION: Palearctic, central and southern Asia, and North America. Winters Africa, India, south-eastern Asia and South America. HABITAT: Riverine areas, lakes and coasts where vertical sandbanks are available for nesting; outside breeding season also in open areas such as wetlands, grasslands and farmlands. FOOD: Chiefly airborne insects. STATUS: MB and PV; a decline in range and numbers.

Greenfinch
Carduelis chloris (Ligurinus chloris). 15cm.
DISTRIBUTION: Western Palearctic. Most populations are partial migrants, except some in south which are resident or dispersive. HABITAT: Open areas with tall trees, including woodland edges, farmlands and gardens. FOOD: Mainly seeds, some invertebrates in breeding season. STATUS: RB and WV. [European Greenfinch]

Hawfinch
Coccothraustes coccothraustes (Coccothraustes vulgaris). 18cm.
DISTRIBUTION: Palearctic. Partially migratory; reaching southern parts of breeding range and beyond to Near East, Iran, north-western India and central and eastern China. HABITAT: Mainly open deciduous and mixed woodlands, farmlands and scrub. FOOD: Mainly seeds, also buds and shoots, and some invertebrates in breeding season. STATUS: RB and PV. Recent decline in some areas.

Goldfinch
Carduelis carduelis (Carduelis elegans). 12cm.
DISTRIBUTION: Western and central Palearctic. Partially migratory; wintering almost entirely within breeding range with concentrations in southern parts. HABITAT: Woodland edges, hedges, orchards, gardens and in winter also in rough grasslands, waste grounds. FOOD: Chiefly seeds; in breeding season also some insects. STATUS: MB and RB. [European Goldfinch]

Siskin
Carduelis spinus. 12cm.
DISTRIBUTION: Palearctic. Partially to wholly migratory; northern populations moving south to Mediterranean region, south-western Asia, Japan and southern China. HABITAT: Coniferous and mixed woodlands, alder and birch thickets by water courses. FOOD: Chiefly seeds, also in breeding season some invertebrates. STATUS: RB, PV and WV. [Eurasian Siskin]

——————— PLATE 16 ———————

Citril Finch
Serinus citrinella (Chrysomitris citrinella), from south-western Palearctic; included by Thorburn on the basis of a single specimen from Norfolk in January, 1904, but re-identified as the Cape Canary *S. canicollis* and deleted from the British and Irish List in 1994 (BOU, Records Commitee: 21st Report).

Serin
Serinus serinus (Serinus hortulanus). 11.5cm.
DISTRIBUTION: West-central, southern and south-western Palearctic. Populations in centre and south of the range are mainly sedentary, those in north winter south to North Africa and the Middle East. HABITAT: Parks, gardens, and open country with scattered clumps of trees, preferably conifers. FOOD: Seeds and other plant materials; occasionally invertebrates. STATUS: CB from 1967, and PV. [European Serin]

House Sparrow (House-Sparrow)
Passer domesticus. 14-15cm.
DISTRIBUTION: Palearctic and southern Eurasia. Essentially sedentary. Widely introduced and now established on most continents and many oceanic islands. HABITAT: Rarely far from human habitation, especially when livestock are present. FOOD: Chiefly seeds and other plant material, also invertebrates, household scraps, STATUS: Common and widespread RB; some decline in recent years, especially in suburbs.

Tree Sparrow (Tree-Sparrow)
Passer montanus. 14cm.
DISTRIBUTION: Palearctic and southern Asia. Mainly sedentary, with small proportion making short-distances migration to the south. HABITAT: Open woodlands, plains, farms, towns. FOOD: Chiefly seeds, also other plant materials and invertebrates. STATUS: RB and PV; serious decline since 1987. ***UK Red Listed***. [Eurasian Tree Sparrow]

Chaffinch
Fringilla coelebs. 14.5cm.
DISTRIBUTION: Western and central Palearctic. Sedentary to migratory, wintering mainly within breeding range in Europe, but further south in Asia. HABITAT: Woodlands, forests, farmlands and urban areas. FOOD: Chiefly invertebrates, especially insects in breeding season; mainly seeds at other times. STATUS: Common RB, and Pv and WV.

Brambling
Fringilla montifringilla. 14cm.
DISTRIBUTION: Northern Eurasia. Winters almost entirely south of breeding range as far as north-western Africa, northern Mediterranean region, Near East east to India and southern China. HABITAT: Mainly open birch-conifer woodlands, riparian willows, farmlands. FOOD: Chiefly seeds and berries, and in summer, insects. STATUS: CB since 1920 in small numbers, PV and WV.

Linnet
Carduelis cannabina (Linota cannabina). 13.5cm.
DISTRIBUTION: Western and central Palearctic. Partially migratory, most moving south to winter within or just beyond breeding range.

HABITAT: Open scrub and heath, cultivated areas with bushes, young plantations and woodland edges. FOOD: Chiefly seeds, some invertebrates. STATUS: MB and RB (recent marked decline), also PV and WV. *UK Red Listed*. [Eurasian Linnet]

Redpoll (Mealy Redpoll)
Carduelis flammea (Linota linaria). 11.5-14.5cm.
DISTRIBUTION: Palearctic and northern North America. Short-distance and long-distance migrant; winters in southern parts of breeding range and beyond to northern Mediterranean region, central Asia, and central USA. HABITAT: Open woodlands, heathlands, scrub/waste lands, gardens, by rivers. FOOD: Chiefly small seeds; invertebrates mainly in breeding season. STATUS: RB and MB (race *C.f.cabaret*, also PV and WV (races *C.f.flammea* and *C.f.rostrata*). [Common Redpoll]

Thorburn's Mealy Redpoll
Linota linaria, is now considered to be merely the race *C.f.flammea*; his **Lesser Redpoll** *Linota rufescens* is now considered to be the race *C.f.caberet*; his **Greenland Redpoll** *Linota rostrata* (plate 80B) is now considered to be the race *C.f.rostrata* which breeds on Baffin Island and Greenland and a pair closely resembling this race bred in Inverness in 1959, also occurs in small numbers as PV and WV.

——————— PLATE 17 ———————

Snow-Finch
Montifringilla nivalis, from the mountains of southern Eurasia, was included by Thorburn on the basis of two specimens, one from Rye Harbour, Sussex, 1905 and another from Paddock Wood, Kent, 1906 ('Hastings Rarities') but this record is no longer accepted for the British-Irish List; the species is however, included as category D1, i.e., there is a reasonable doubt that it has ever occurred in a wild state.

Twite
Carduelis flavirostris (Linota flavirostris). 14cm.
DISTRIBUTION: Eurasia. Sedentary to wholly migratory; moving to lower elevations, and further south in south-eastward direction to northern continental Europe. HABITAT: Open, arid and stony ground with sparse bushes; outside breeding season seashores, salt-marshes and coastal fields. FOOD: chiefly seeds. STATUS: RB and MB, also PV and WV. Some decline. *UK Red Listed*. [Common Linnet]

Bullfinch
Pyrrhula pyrrhula (Pyrrhula europaea). 14.5-16.5cm.
DISTRIBUTION: Eurasia. Essentially resident though some move south of breeding range to northern Mediterranean region, east to Korea and central and north-eastern China and Japan. HABITAT: Deciduous, coniferous and mixed forests and woodlands, farmlands, gardens, orchards. FOOD: Chiefly seeds of fleshy fruits, buds and shoots; some invertebrates. STATUS: RB and few SV. Serious decline. *UK Red Listed*. [Eurasian or Common Bullfinch]

Common Rosefinch (Scarlet Grosbeak)
Carpodacus erythrinus (Pyrrhula erythrina). 14.5-15cm.
DISTRIBUTION: Eurasia. Winters India, south-eastern Asia and southern China. HABITAT: Thickets, riparian woodlands and scrub, farmlands, gardens. In winter in open forests, scrub jungle, bushes in cultivated areas. FOOD: Seeds, buds and other plant parts; some invertebrates. STATUS: CB and regular PV.

Pine Grosbeak
Pinicola enucleator (Pyrrhula enucleator). 18.5cm.
DISTRIBUTION: Northern Eurasia and western and northern North America. Mainly resident with some irregular southward movements in winter. HABITAT: Coniferous and deciduous forests. In winter often in towns. FOOD: Buds, shoots and seeds; invertebrates in breeding season. STATUS: SV.

Crossbill
Loxia curvirostra. 16.5cm.
DISTRIBUTION: Palearctic, northern Philippines, North and Middle America. Resident and dispersive, also irregularly eruptive. HABITAT: Conifers in forests, woodlands, parks, gardens. FOOD: Chiefly conifer seeds. STATUS: Fluctuates widely; RB and MB, WV and SV. [Red Crossbill]

Two-barred Crossbill
Loxia leucoptera (Loxia bifasciata). 15cm.
DISTRIBUTION: Northern Eurasia, western and northern North America, also Hispaniola. Mainly resident, but some eruptive and dispersive movements dependent on conifer seed crop. HABITAT: Coniferous forests, mixed woodlands. FOOD: Chiefly conifer seeds. STATUS: Irregular SV. [White-winged Crossbill]

Black-headed Bunting
Emberiza melanocephala. 16-17cm.
DISTRIBUTION: South-central Eurasia. Winters in western and central India. HABITAT: Open areas with scattered bushes, trees and hedges, mainly in arable land, especially in winter. FOOD: Chiefly seeds and other plant material; insects in breeding season. STATUS: SV, mostly April to November.

Pine Bunting (Pine-Bunting)
Emberiza leucocephalos (Emberiza leucocephala). 16.5cm.
DISTRIBUTION: Eastern Asia. Winters south to Middle East, northern Pakistan, north-western India, central China and Korea. HABITAT: Open woodlands, forest edges, bushes, often near water. FOOD: Chiefly seeds and other plant material; insects in breeding season. Status: Irregular SV. See also Plate 80B

Corn Bunting (Corn-Bunting)
Miliaria calandra (Emberiza miliaria). 18cm.
DISTRIBUTION: Western and southern Palearctic. Resident to partially migratory, Wintering mainly within breeding range. HABITAT: Open country, often cultivated areas, such as arable farmlands, grasslands and scrub. FOOD: Chiefly seeds, also invertebrates, especially in breeding season. STATUS: RB, PV and WV. Large decline. *UK Red Listed*.

——————— PLATE 18 ———————

Yellow-breasted Bunting
Emberiza aureola. 14-15cm.
DISTRIBUTION: Northern and eastern Eurasia. Winters from India east to south-eastern Asia. HABITAT: Willow and birch thickets, marshy scrub, bushy fields near streams. FOOD: Chiefly seeds and other plant material, also insects in breeding season. STATUS: SV, mainly August to October.

Yellowhammer (Yellow Bunting or Yellow Hammer)
Emberiza citrinella. 16-16.5cm.
DISTRIBUTION: Eurasia. Sedentary to migratory, but mostly a partial migrant, wintering largely within and south of breeding range. HABITAT: Open country, especially cultivated areas with hedges, plantations, scrub, rough grasslands and parklands. FOOD: Chiefly seeds, also invertebrates mainly in breeding season. STATUS: RB, PV and WV. Declining. [Yellow-Hammer]

Cirl Bunting
Emberiza cirlus. 15.5cm.
DISTRIBUTION: Western Palearctic. Mainly sedentary. HABITAT: Heath, scrub and agriculture areas, especially small weedy fields, dense hedges. FOOD: Chiefly seeds, also invertebrates in summer. STATUS: RB but large decline in range and numbers. *UK Red Listed*.

Ortolan Bunting (Ortolan)
Emberiza hortulana. 16-17cm.
DISTRIBUTION: Western Eurasia. Winters in Arabia and sahel zone south

of Sahara. HABITAT: Open country with few trees and shrubs, in farmlands, rocky meadows, grasslands, olive orchards and forest clearings. FOOD: Probably mainly invertebrates and seeds, especially outside breeding season. STATUS: Regular, scarce PV.

Rock Bunting (Meadow-Bunting)
Emberiza cia. 16cm.
DISTRIBUTION: Southern Palearctic. Mainly resident though some winter at lower altitudes. HABITAT: Open ground with sparse shrub vegetation in rocky areas and forest edges. Outside breeding season in open country at lower altitudes. FOOD: Chiefly seeds and other plant material; also invertebrates in breeding season. STATUS: SV.

Meadow Bunting (Siberian Meadow-Bunting)
Emberiza cioides, from eastern Asia, was included by Thorburn based on a specimen from Flamborough, Yorkshire, 1886. One of the 'Hastings rarities' and no longer accepted in the British-Irish List.

Rustic Bunting
Emberiza rustica. 14.5-15.5cm.
DISTRIBUTION: Northern Eurasia. Winters mainly in eastern China and Japan. HABITAT: Bushes and wet grassy areas in taiga, undergrowth of mixed woodlands, thickets by streams. FOOD: Mainly seeds; also insects and spiders in breeding season. STATUS: SV.

Little Bunting
Emberiza pusilla. 13-14cm.
DISTRIBUTION: Northern Eurasia. Winters from Turkestan to south-eastern Asia and southern China. HABITAT: Birch and willow scrub, undergrowth in taiga. In winter found in bracken and short grass on hillsides; also stubble fields. FOOD: Chiefly seeds; also invertebrates in breeding season. STATUS: Annual, mainly autumn, SV.

Reed Bunting (Reed-Bunting)
Emberiza schoeniclus. 15-16cm.
DISTRIBUTION: Eurasia. Sedentary to migratory; northern populations winter in southern parts of breeding range and beyond to northern Africa, Iraq, India, southern China and southern Japan. HABITAT: Mainly reedbeds, marshes, riverbanks and in winter in farmlands, coastal scrub, marshes. FOOD: Chiefly seeds and other plant materials; mainly invertebrates in breeding season. STATUS: RB, PV and WV. Large decline. **UK Red Listed**.

Lapland Bunting
Calcarius lapponicus. 15-16cm.
DISTRIBUTION: Northern Palearctic and northern North America. Winters south to central Europe, southern Russia, Mongolia, China, Korea, Japan, and northern and central USA. HABITAT: Wet meadows, grassy tussocks, tundra scrub. In winter on grassy areas bordering coasts and estuaries, grass moorlands, stubble fields. FOOD: Chiefly seeds in winter; invertebrates in breeding season. STATUS: CB, PV and WV. Lapland Longspur]

Snow Bunting (Snow-Bunting)
Plectrophenax nivalis. 16-17cm.
DISTRIBUTION: Northern Palearctic and northern North America. Partially migratory to migratory; winters south to central USA, north-western and central Europe, southern Russia, central Asia and Japan. HABITAT: Arctic rocky shores, cliffs, dry tundra, mountain tops. In winter on moors, farmlands, coastal stubble, salt-marshes. FOOD: Mainly seeds, also invertebrates in the breeding season.

STATUS: RB (small numbers), PV and WV.

——————————— PLATE 19 ———————————

Starling
Sturnus vulgaris. 21.5cm.
DISTRIBUTION: Palearctic. Migratory and resident; winters within breeding range and beyond to Iberia, north Africa, and southern Asia east to India. Widely introduced. HABITAT: Most areas from farmlands and woodlands and also to large cities. FOOD: Omnivorous, animal food predominating in breeding season. STATUS: RB, PV and WV; common but some decline in recent years. [Common Starling]

Rose-coloured Starling
Sturnus roseus (Pastor roseus). 21.5cm.
DISTRIBUTION: South-central Eurasia. Nomadic wanderer, irruptive migrant and migratory; winters mainly in India and Sri Lanka. HABITAT: Dry, open, often arid areas, grasslands and rocky terrain. In winter quarters in open farmlands. FOOD: In breeding season mainly insects; otherwise fruits, nectar and seeds. STATUS: Almost annual SV. [Rosy Starling]

Chough
Pyrrhocorax pyrrhocorax (Pyrrhocorax graculus). 39-40cm.
DISTRIBUTION: Palearctic and north-eastern Ethiopia. Essentially sedentary. HABITAT: Mainly in remote stony mountain and rocky coastal areas, with natural and semi-natural, grazed pastures. FOOD: Soil-living insects and other invertebrate; also seeds and fruit. STATUS: RB in small numbers. [Red-billed Chough]

Nutcracker
Nucifraga caryocatactes. 30-33cm.
DISTRIBUTION: Eurasia. Resident and eruptive dependent on conifer seed crop. HABITAT: Coniferous and mixed woodlands dominated by conifers. FOOD: Conifer seeds, nuts and berries, invertebrates and sometimes small vertebrates. Winter diet of sedentary birds almost wholly seeds and nuts. STATUS: SV. [Spotted Nutcracker]

Jay
Garrulus glandarius. 34-35cm.
DISTRIBUTION: Palearctic and northern Oriental. Sedentary in west and south of range, eruptive migrant in east and north. HABITAT: Deciduous, coniferous and mixed woodlands, orchards, parks, gardens. FOOD: Omnivorous, including carrion and domestic scraps. STATUS: RB and some WV. [Eurasian Jay]

——————————— PLATE 20 ———————————

Magpie
Pica pica (Pica rustica). 44-46cm.
DISTRIBUTION: Palearctic and western North America. Essentially sedentary. HABITAT: Open woodland, scrub, savanna, farmlands grassland with dense hedges, scattered trees and bushes, gardens, parks. FOOD: Omnivorous, including carrion, refuse and scraps. Chiefly insects in spring and summer; vertebrates, fruits and seeds in autumn and winter. STATUS: Common and widespread RB. [Black-billed Magpie]

Jackdaw
Corvus monedula. 33-34cm.
DISTRIBUTION: Palearctic. Resident to migratory; wintering almost entirely within breeding range. HABITAT: Mature woodlands, parks, cliffs and city buildings with access to open ground for feeding. FOOD: Omnivorous, including carrion and scraps. STATUS: Common RB, and WV. [Eurasian Jackdaw]

Raven
Corvus corax. 64cm.
DISTRIBUTION: Palearctic and Nearctic. Mainly sedentary. HABITAT: Many types of country, most often in open, mountainous or coastal regions. FOOD: Omnivorous, including carrion and refuse. STATUS: RB in west and north. [Common Raven]

————— PLATE 21 —————

Carrion Crow/Hooded Crow (Carrion-Crow)
Corvus corone (Corvus corone and Corvus cornix). 45-47cm.
DISTRIBUTION: Eurasia. Northern populations are partially to wholly migratory, wintering in southern parts of breeding range and beyond to northern India and southern China. HABITAT: Almost all habitats except dense and extensive forests. FOOD: Omnivorous, principally invertebrates and cereal; also carrion and scraps. STATUS: Common and widespread RB and WV. Carrion Crow (race corone) and Hooded Crow (race cornix in British isles) are different races of a single species.

Rook
Corvus frugilegus. 44-46cm.
DISTRIBUTION: Eurasia. Resident to migratory; winters within and south of breeding range. HABITAT: Open country, farmlands, parks and pastures with trees, woodlands. FOOD: Invertebrates, especially insects and earthworms, plant materials, mainly cereal grain, small vertebrates, carrion and scraps. STATUS: Common RB and WV.

————— PLATE 22 —————

Skylark (Sky-lark)
Alauda arvensis. 18-19cm.
DISTRIBUTION: Palearctic. Wholly migratory southwards in north and east of breeding range grading to local movements in south. HABITAT: Mainly open grasslands or low green herbage. FOOD: Plant and animal material; chiefly invertebrates, especially insects in breeding season, seeds, grain and leaves at other times. STATUS: RB, PV and WV. Large decline. *UK Red Listed.* [Eurasian Skylark or Sky Lark]

Woodlark (Wood-Lark)
Lullula arborea (Alauda arborea). 15cm.
DISTRIBUTION: Western Palearctic. Partially migratory, wintering in the western and southern parts of breeding range. HABITAT: Open bare ground intermingled with short grass and areas of longer vegetation with some trees or bushes. FOOD: Insects and spiders during breeding season, chiefly seeds at other times. STATUS: RB or MB; large reduction in range since 1960s. *UK Red Listed.* [Wood Lark]

Crested Lark
Galerida cristata (Alauda cristata). 17cm.
DISTRIBUTION: Palearctic, sub-Saharan Africa. Mainly resident except in northern Russia, where it is migratory. HABITAT: Open, dry, flat or gently sloping lowland areas with low or sparse vegetation. FOOD: Plant materials, mainly seeds, and invertebrates, mainly beetles. STATUS: Irregular SV.

Short-toed Lark
Calandrella brachydactyla (Alauda brachydactyla). 13-14cm.
DISTRIBUTION: Southern Palearctic. Chiefly migratory, wintering in Africa south to the Sahel and Red Sea, and southern Asia east to India. HABITAT: Mainly dry, open plains and uplands, terraces, slopes and undulating hills. FOOD: Insects and seeds in summer, mostly seeds only at other times. STATUS: Annual SV. [Greater Short-toed Lark]

White-winged Lark
Melanocorypha leucoptera (Alauda sibirica). 18cm.
Distribution: Central Eurasia. Short-distance migrant, south and west to the Black Sea and Rumania. HABITAT: Chiefly dry plains with short vegetation, shores of freshwater and salt lakes. In winter in forest-steppe. FOOD: Insects and seeds in summer, seeds in winter. STATUS: SV.

Black Lark
Melanocorypha yeltoniensis (Alauda yeltoniensis), from central Asia, which Thorburn included based on four specimens from the Sussex/Kent borders, 1907. They were part of the 'Hastings Rarities' and are no longer accepted in the British-Irish List.

Shore Lark
Eremophila alpestris (Otocrys alpestris). 14-17cm.
DISTRIBUTION: Palearctic, west-central China and Nearctic to central and eastern Colombia. Northern races migratory, southern races resident or make altitudinal movements. HABITAT: Dry tundra, sandy or stony ground, and wide variety of open habitats in Nearctic. In winter, coastal dunes, salt-marshes, beaches and arable land. FOOD: In summer, insects and some seeds; in winter, seeds. STATUS: CB (Scotland 1973-77), and WV. [Horned Lark]

————— PLATE 23 —————

Swift
Apus apus (Cypselus apus). 16-17cm.
DISTRIBUTION: Eurasia. Winters in Africa, south of the Sahara. HABITAT: All activity is aerial and underlying terrain is of secondary relevance. Nests in cliffs, caves, buildings, and in east, also in trees. FOOD: Chiefly flying insects and airborne spiders. STATUS: Common MB and PV. [Common Swift]

Alpine Swift
Apus melba (Cypselus melba). 20-22cm.
DISTRIBUTION: Palearctic, east to India, and eastern and southern Africa, Madagascar. Northern populations winter south to tropical Africa and India. HABITAT: Almost exclusively aerial, and underlying terrain only significant for pattern of air currents and quantity of airborne food. Nests in cliffs, caves, trees and buildings. FOOD: Flying insects and spiders. STATUS: Annual SV. [*Tachymarptis melba*]

Needle-tailed Swift
Hirundapus caudacutus (Acanthyllis caudacuta). 19-20cm.
DISTRIBUTION: Eastern and southern Asia. Winters in Australia. HABITAT: Entirely aerial, apart from roosting and nesting in holes and crevices of rocks or trees. FOOD: Airborne insects and spiders. STATUS: SV. [White-throated Needletail]

Nightjar
Caprimulgus europaeus. 26-28cm.
DISTRIBUTION: Palearctic. Winters in tropical and southern Africa. HABITAT: Dry, open areas, in heathlands, woodland edges and clearings, young conifer plantations. FOOD: Flying insects, mainly moths and beetles. STATUS: MB and PV. Declining in numbers and range. *UK Red Listed.* [Eurasian or European Nightjar]

Red-necked Nightjar
Caprimulgus ruficollis. 30-32cm.
DISTRIBUTION: South-western Palearctic. Migratory but winter quarters in West Africa not yet delineated. HABITAT: Requires patches of bare or sandy soil, scattered ground cover, and some bushes or trees; in conifer woods, oak scrub, olive or Eucalyptus groves. FOOD: Insects, mostly in flight but some from ground. STATUS: SV (1 record 1856).

Egyptian Nightjar
Caprimulgus aegyptius. 24-26cm.
DISTRIBUTION: South-western and south-central Palearctic. Winters in Sahel zone below Sahara and north-eastern Africa. HABITAT: Prefers low

sand-dunes with sparse trees and herbage or low-lying hot deserts or semi-desert, locally adjacent to water. FOOD: Insects. STATUS: SV.

———————— PLATE 24 ————————

Wryneck
Jynx torquilla (Iynx torquilla). 16-17cm.
DISTRIBUTION: Palearctic. Winters south to central Africa, India, south-eastern Asia southern China and southern Japan. HABITAT: Variety of forest types, neither dense nor tall, from open woodlands, forest margins, orchards and parks. In winter in scrub, semi-deserts and cultivated areas. FOOD: Chiefly ants (all stages); also other insects. STATUS: FB, CB and PV. Large decline and now almost extinct (1-6pairs). *UK Red Listed*. [Eurasian Wryneck]

Green Woodpecker
Picus viridis (Gecinus viridis). 31-33cm.
DISTRIBUTION: Western Eurasia. Resident. HABITAT: Usually semi-open landscapes with woodlands, hedgerows, scattered old trees, forest edges and flood-plain forests, orchards, parklands; all with nearby open grassy areas suitable for foraging. FOOD: Chiefly adult and pupal ants. STATUS: Common RB. [Eurasian Green Woodpecker]

Great Spotted Woodpecker
Dendrocopus major. 22-23cm.
DISTRIBUTION: Palearctic. Basically resident. HABITAT: Deciduous, coniferous and mixed woodlands, copses, gardens. FOOD: Mainly insects, also bird eggs and nestlings in summer and tree seeds in winter. STATUS: Common and widespread RB, and some PV and WV.

Lesser Spotted Woodpecker
Dendrocopus minor. 14-15cm.
DISTRIBUTION: Paleartcic. Basically resident. HABITAT: Deciduous, open woodlands, edges, river banks, parklands, orchards, gardens. FOOD: Chiefly insects. STATUS: RB, but declining from ca.1980.

Kingfisher
Alcedo atthis (Alcedo ispida). 16-17cm.
DISTRIBUTION: Palearctic, southern Asia, Indonesia and New Guinea region. Shows progression from mainly resident or dispersive in west of range, to partially migratory in centre and migratory in north and east. HABITAT: Requires clear, unpolluted water, preferably still or gently flowing. Outside breeding season also in ice-free estuaries, larger lakes and coastlines. FOOD: Chiefly fish, also aquatic insects, and occasionally crustaceans, molluscs and amphibians. STATUS: RB and MB; some recent decline. [Common Kingfisher]

Roller
Coracias garrulus. 30-32cm.
DISTRIBUTION: Palearctic. Winters in Afrotropical region, mainly in eastern and southeastern Africa. HABITAT: Open meadows and steppe, with scattered, mature trees, also tree-lined river banks and orchards. In winter quarters favours dry bushy country with dead trees. FOOD: Chiefly insects. STATUS: Almost annual SV. [European Roller]

———————— PLATE 25 ————————

Bee-eater
Merops apiaster. 27-29cm.
DISTRIBUTION: Southern Palearctic and southern Africa. Winters mainly in western, eastern and southern Africa. HABITAT: Sunny warm open areas with scattered trees, in sheltered valleys and lowlands; pasture, grasslands, open fields, steppe plains or river banks. In winter occupies savannas, plains, grasslands, dry forests, lake shores, river banks and cultivated areas. FOOD: Flying insects, especially

bees and wasps. STATUS: CB and almost annual PV. [European Bee-eater]

Hoopoe
Upupa epops. 26-28cm.
DISTRIBUTION: Palearctic, west-central and northern central Africa, and southern Asia. Migratory in northern parts of range; wintering mainly in sub-Saharan Africa and southern Asia. HABITAT: Requires warm, dry, level or gently undulating terrain with bare surfaces; savannas, steppes, open woodland clearings, meadows, farmlands, towns. FOOD: Chiefly insects, especially their larvae and pupae. STATUS: CB and annual, mainly spring, PV. [Eurasian Hoopoe]

Cuckoo
Cuculus canorus. 32-34cm.
DISTRIBUTION: Palearctic. Winters in southern Africa and south-eastern Asia south to Philippines. HABITAT: Woodlands, open country with scattered trees in farmlands, parks, reedbeds, heaths, coastal dunes or marshes. FOOD: Chiefly insects, especially caterpillars. STATUS: MB and PV. [Common Cuckoo]

Great Spotted Cuckoo
Clamator glandarius (Coccystes glandarius). 38-40cm.
DISTRIBUTION: Southwestern Palearctic and Africa. Migratory at northern and southern ends of breeding range, but in between is resident or makes short-distance movements. HABITAT: Heathlands, open woodlands, thorn-scrub, olive groves. FOOD: Chiefly insects, especially caterpillars. STATUS: Irregular SV.

Yellow-billed Cuckoo (American Yellow-billed Cuckoo)
Coccyzus americanus. 28-32cm.
DISTRIBUTION: North America, northern Mexico and Greater Antilles. Winters mainly in South America south to Argentina. HABITAT: Open woodlands, dense secondary growth in rural areas, deserted farmlands, and thickets near watercourses. In winter also in rain forest clearings. FOOD: Chiefly insects, especially caterpillars. STATUS: Irregular, mainly autumn, SV.

———————— PLATE 26 ————————

Barn Owl (Barn-Owl)
Tyto alba (Strix flammea). 33-35cm.
DISTRIBUTION: Almost cosmopolitan. Basically resident, though some northern populations partially migratory. HABITAT: Mainly in open areas of rough grasslands and marshes, farmlands or forests with grassland corridors. Uses mainly buildings, tree-holes, and cliff crevices, for nesting and roosting. FOOD: Chiefly small mammals, also birds amphibians, fish and insects. STATUS: RB and some SV. Major decline over past 100 years.

Long-eared Owl
Asio otus. 35-37cm.
DISTRIBUTION: Palearctic and western and central North America. Northern populations mainly migratory, wintering chiefly within southern two-thirds of breeding range and beyond to Levant, southern Asia and northern Mexico. HABITAT: Open spaces with short herbage near-by, usually small, coniferous, mixed or deciduous woodlands, also, especially in winter, salt-marshes, moorlands, heathlands. FOOD: Chiefly small mammals. STATUS: RB, PV and WV.

Short-eared Owl
Asio flammeus (Asio accipitrinus). 37-39cm.
DISTRIBUTION: Northern and central Eurasia, North America, Greater Antilles, central Pacific islands and South America. Migratory in north to partially migratory and resident; wintering south to Mexico, northern Afrotropics, Middle East, Indian subcontinent and south-east Asia. HABITAT: Open areas such as marshes, bogs, moorlands, meadows,

alpine heaths, sand-dunes, and forest clearings. In winter also in coastal lowlands and rough farmlands and cultivated land. FOOD: Chiefly small mammals. STATUS: RB, MB, PV and WV. Fluctuating numbers, related to prey abundance.

Tawny Owl
Strix aluco (Syrnium aluco). 37-39cm.
DISTRIBUTION: Palearctic and southern Asia. Sedentary. HABITAT: Deciduous and coniferous woodlands and orchards, and other wooded cultivated and urban areas. FOOD: Chiefly small mammals, also birds, amphibians, insects and earthworms. STATUS: Widespread RB. Possibly some small decline.

———————————— PLATE 27 ————————————

Tengmalm's Owl
Aegolius funereus (Nyctala tengmalmi). 24-26cm.
DISTRIBUTION: Palearctic, northern and west-central North America. Largely resident or dispersive; northern populations occasionally eruptive, linked to mammal prey densities. HABITAT: Chiefly deciduous and mixed forests; hunts also in near-by meadows and moors. FOOD: Chiefly small rodents and birds. STATUS: Irregular SV. [Boreal Owl]

Little Owl
Athene noctua. 21-23cm.
DISTRIBUTION: Palearctic and northern African region. Resident. HABITAT: Forest edges and clearings, open deciduous woodlands, agriculture land, old orchards, urban areas, elevated steppe and semi-desert. FOOD: Chiefly small mammals and birds, insects and earthworms. STATUS: IB and SV. Introduced 19th century. Declining in range and numbers.

Snowy Owl
Nyctea scandiaca. 53-66cm.
DISTRIBUTION: Northern Palearctic and northern North America. Partially migratory and nomadic; also eruptive at times, related to food abundance. HABITAT: Alpine mountain heaths and in tundra areas above tree-line. FOOD: Chiefly rodents, mainly lemmings and voles; also other mammals and birds. STATUS: CB (Fetlar, Scotland, 1967-1975) and irregular SV.

Hawk Owl (Hawk-Owl)
Surnia ulula (Surnia funerea). 36-39cm.
DISTRIBUTION: Northern Eurasia and northern North America. Dispersive and occasionally eruptive. HABITAT: Fringes of forest tundra and boreal taiga, south to edge of forest steppe and cultivated lands. FOOD: Chiefly small voles; also some birds and larger mammals. STATUS: Irregular SV. [Northern Hawk Owl]

Scops Owl (Scops-Owl)
Otus scops (Scops giu). 19-20cm.
DISTRIBUTION: Palearctic, eastern Asia and Malayan Archipelagos and African region. Northern populations migratory, wintering mainly northern Afrotropics, southern Asia to Japan and southern Sumatra; southern populations partially migratory or resident. HABITAT: Open woodlands, riverine forests, cultivated land with trees, orchards, olive-groves, parks and gardens. In winter, varied habitats but usually where there are dense clumps of bushes. FOOD: Chiefly insects and other invertebrates. STATUS: Irregular SV. [Common or Eurasian Scops-Owl]

———————————— PLATE 28 ————————————

Eagle Owl (Eagle-Owl)
Bubo bubo (Bubo ignavus): though Thorburn included this species, the conclusion of an extensive review published in 1996 removed it from the official British and Irish List. The Records Committee of the British Ornithologists' Union agreed in their 23rd Report (Ibis 139: 197-201) that because of the possibility of escapes, releases and confusion over the provenance of skins, there was no evidence that this species had occurred in the wild state in Britain or Ireland for over 200 years and it should not therefore be included in the Checklist of Birds of Britain and Ireland. [Eurasian Eagle-Owl]

———————————— PLATE 29 ————————————

Griffon Vulture (Griffon-Vulture)
Gyps fulvus. 95-105cm.
DISTRIBUTION: Southern Palearctic. Resident and partially migratory. HABITAT: Open country with few or no trees, in plains, mountains or upland plateaux. FOOD: Carrion, usually domestic livestock. STATUS: SV. [Eurasian Griffon or Eurasian Griffon Vulture]

Egyptian Vulture
Neophron percnopterus. 60-70cm.
DISTRIBUTION: Southern Palearctic and northern and north-eastern Africa. Sedentary and migratory; wintering mainly in Sahel zone of Africa and in India. HABITAT: Open areas such as steppes, savannas and river banks. Nests mainly in cliffs or crags. FOOD: Mainly carrion and organic rubbish. STATUS: SV.

———————————— PLATE 30 ————————————

Marsh Harrier (Marsh-Harrier)
Circus aeruginosus. 48-56cm.
DISTRIBUTION: Central Palearctic, Madagascar, central and eastern New Guinea, Australasian region and south-western Oceania. Sedentary and migratory; Eurasian populations mostly winter south to central and south-eastern Africa east through southern Asia to China and the Philippines. HABITAT: Shallow, standing, fresh or brackish waters fringed by tall emergent aquatics; swamps, marshes, grasslands. FOOD: Chiefly small mammals, birds and carrion. STATUS: Small numbers MB or RB, and scarce PV. ***UK Red Listed***. [Includes: Western Marsh-Harrier, Eastern Marsh-Harrier, Madagascar Marsh-Harrier and Swamp Harrier]

Hen Harrier (Hen-Harrier)
Circus cyaneus. 44-52cm.
DISTRIBUTION: Eurasia and northern North America. Partially migratory or locally resident, though migratory in north and north-eastern Eurasia and northern North America, moving south as far as Mediterranean region, southern Asia, south-eastern China and Central America. HABITAT: Wide range of dry or damp, open terrain with low vegetation; prairies, moors, marshes, steppe and fields. FOOD: Chiefly birds and small rodents. STATUS: Small numbers RB, MB, PV and WV. UK Red Listed. [Northern Harrier]

Montagu's Harrier
Circus pygargus (Circus cineraceus). 43-47cm.
DISTRIBUTION: Western and central Palearctic. Winters principally in savannas of tropical and eastern Africa, and Indian subcontinent. HABITAT: Basically in lowlands, mainly in broad river valleys, plains and levels adjacent to lakes or seas; heathlands, rough grasslands, dunes, cereal fields, young conifer plantations. FOOD: Chiefly birds and small mammals, also lizards and insects. STATUS: Small numbers MB (7 pairs, 1995), and PV.

———————————— PLATE 31 ————————————

Buzzard (Common Buzzard)
Buteo buteo (Buteo vulgaris). 51-57cm.
DISTRIBUTION: Palearctic. Island races resident; western and south-

eastern populations resident or short-distance migrants; eastern populations long-distance migrants, wintering south to Arabia and eastern Africa, India and China. HABITAT: Mountains, moors, heaths, wooded farmlands, coastal cliffs. FOOD: Chiefly small mammals, also birds, reptiles, amphibians, insects and earthworms. STATUS: RB, some increase. [Common Buzzard]

Rough-legged Buzzard
Buteo lagopus. 50-60cm.
DISTRIBUTION: Northern Eurasia and northern North America. Winters south mainly to central Eurasia and northern USA. HABITAT: Largely in treeless tundra or upland areas, and at all seasons prefers open terrain with rough low-growing vegetation. In winter in more temperate regions, often where cultivated or settled. FOOD: Chiefly small mammals. STATUS: Normally scarce PV and WV, but periodically in greater numbers. [Rough-legged Hawk]

Spotted Eagle
Aquila clanga (Aquila maculata). 65-72cm.
DISTRIBUTION: Central Eurasia. Migratory and partially migratory; wintering mainly around eastern Mediterranean, Middle East, east Africa and southern Asia, east to south-eastern Asia. HABITAT: Mainly in lowland forests bordering water bodies or wetlands. FOOD: Chiefly small vertebrates, especially mammals, insects and carrion. STATUS: Irregular SV; last recorded 1915. *Global Conservation Concern.* [Greater Spotted Eagle]

―――――――――― PLATE 32 ――――――――――

Golden Eagle
Aquila chrysaetos (Aquila chrysaetus). 75-88cm.
DISTRIBUTION: Palearctic and Nearctic. Resident and dispersive in western Palearctic, with migratory movements south in eastern Siberia and North America. HABITAT: Typically in mountainous landscapes where tree cover is sparse or fragmented, also in lowland wooded peatlands or wetland terrain. FOOD: Chiefly mammals and birds, alive or dead, also reptiles. STATUS: RB, mainly in Scotland.

―――――――――― PLATE 33 ――――――――――

White-tailed Eagle
Haliaeetus albicilla. 70-90cm.
DISTRIBUTION: Palearctic and south-western Alaska. Resident, dispersive or migratory according to latitude and age-class; wholly migratory north of 60° N, and juveniles and immatures wander extensively. HABITAT: Always associated with wetlands and coasts. FOOD: Chiefly fish and carrion, also waterbirds. STATUS: FB, IB (10 pairs, 1995), and SV; re-introduced since 1975. *UK Red Listed.*

Osprey
Pandion haliaetus. 55-58cm.
DISTRIBUTION: Nearly cosmopolitan, though does not breed in South America. Migratory and sedentary, northern populations wintering south to Mediterranean, Africa, India, Philippines, Sundas and South America. HABITAT: Along coasts and in forests close to fresh, brackish and salt water with sufficient fish supplies. FOOD: Primarily fish. STATUS: MB and PV. Extinct as British breeder from 1916 to 1955 when started to nest again in Scotland. *UK Red Listed.*

―――――――――― PLATE 34 ――――――――――

Goshawk
Accipiter gentilis (Astur palumbarius). 48-62cm.
DISTRIBUTION: Palearctic and North America. Partially migratory in arctic and subarctic, dispersive (markedly southwards for Nearctic race) or resident further south. HABITAT: Coniferous, deciduous or mixed forests and woodlands, especially those interspersed with fields or wetlands. FOOD: Chiefly birds and mammals. STATUS: FB, IB, PV and SV. Ceased to breed in 19th century; regular breeding rediscovered from 1968, probably due to escapes and releases of falconer's birds. [Northern Goshawk]

Sparrowhawk
Accipiter nisus. 28-38cm.
DISTRIBUTION: Palearctic. Migratory, partially migratory and dispersive. Extent of regular seasonal movement increases progressively to north and north-east; winters within breeding range or beyond, mainly to Asia. HABITAT: Well-grown, undisturbed woodlands with adjoining, partly open terrain which has cover. FOOD: Chiefly birds. STATUS: RB, PV and WV. Increasing after decline of 1950s and 1960s. [Eurasian Sparrowhawk]

―――――――――― PLATE 35 ――――――――――

Red Kite (Kite)
Milvus milvus (Milvus ictinus). 60-66cm.
DISTRIBUTION: Western Palearctic. Mainly migratory in north and central Europe; resident and dispersive further south, wintering predominantly in the Mediterranean basin. HABITAT: Lowland areas or mountain valleys with large open areas close to woodlands. FOOD: Chiefly carrion, also small vertebrates, especially mammals and birds, and invertebrates. STATUS: Small number RB, PV and WV: re-introduction began 1989. *UK Red Listed.*

Black Kite
Milvus migrans. 55-60cm.
DISTRIBUTION: Old World, African region and Australia. Mainly migratory, though some southern Eurasian and Australian populations largely resident or nomadic; migrations chiefly south of Sahara in tropical Africa, Indian subcontinent, south-eastern Asia. HABITAT: Lowland areas or mountain valleys, often near water courses and lakes, also where livestock-rearing occurs, rubbish dumps, and towns. FOOD: Chiefly carrion and wide range of mainly animal species. STATUS: Increasingly regular SV.

Honey Buzzard (Honey-Buzzard)
Pernis apivorus. 52-60cm.
DISTRIBUTION: Western and central Eurasia. Winters south of the Sahara, mainly in western and central tropical Africa. HABITAT: Favours secluded forests interspersed with clearings and open ground. FOOD: Chiefly social Hymenoptera in summer and winter quarters; also, and more so in spring, other invertebrates, amphibians, reptiles, small mammals and birds. STATUS: Small number MB (4-23 pairs, 1989-93) and few irregular PV. [European Honey-Buzzard]

―――――――― PLATE 36 AND PLATE 37 ――――――――

Gyr Falcon (Greenland Falcon, Iceland Falcon and European Gyrfalcon*)
Falco rusticolus (Falco candicans, Falco islandus and Falco gyrfalco). 50-60cm.
DISTRIBUTION: Northern Palearctic and northern North America. Holarctic. Migratory in high latitudes only; wintering south to Europe, central Asia and northern USA. HABITAT: Cliffs, either coastal or inland, also tree-nesting in some areas. Hunts over open terrain with short or sparse vegetation. FOOD: Chiefly medium-sized birds; also mammals. STATUS: Almost annual SV in very small numbers. [Gyrfalcon]

Now accepted that these are merely colour phases in the regions cited and figured by Thorburn.

Peregrine (Peregrine Falcon)
Falco peregrinus. 36-48cm.
DISTRIBUTION: Almost cosmopolitan. Migratory in north and north-east, grading through strongly dispersive to resident in south and west. HABITAT: Mainly cliffs, crags or other precipitous situations, including man-made tall structures, also tree-tops or on ground. Requires extensive open terrain for hunting. FOOD: Chiefly birds. STATUS: RB or PV, WV and SV: some recent increase. [Peregrine Falcon]

———————— PLATE 38 ————————

Hobby
Falco subbuteo. 30-36cm.
DISTRIBUTION: Palearctic. Winters mainly in southern half of Africa, northern India, Burma and south-eastern China. HABITAT: Open areas, of low vegetation with clumps of tall trees or fringed by woodlands with clearings. In winter prefers savannas, sparse woodlands, grasslands and areas of cultivation. FOOD: Chiefly birds and insects. STATUS: Relatively small numbers MB and PV. [Eurasian Hobby]

Merlin
Falco columbarius (Falco aesalon). 25-30cm.
DISTRIBUTION: Northern Palearctic and North America. Mainly migratory, some resident; wintering south of breeding range to north-western Africa, Mediterranean region, southern and south-eastern Asia, and northern South America. HABITAT: Open terrain with low, rough vegetation on uplands, foothills and plains, including coastal strips, sand-dunes, saltings and wetlands. In winter also farmlands. FOOD: Chiefly small birds. STATUS: RB or MB, PV and WV. Historical decline. ***UK Red Listed***.

Red-footed Falcon
Falco vespertinus. 29-31cm.
DISTRIBUTION: Central Eurasia. Winters mainly in south-western Africa. HABITAT: Open areas, such as grasslands, meadows and bogs fringed or interspersed with stands of trees, also in forest clearings or edges. In winter quarters in savannas, farmlands and dry grasslands. FOOD: Chiefly insects and when breeding small vertebrates. STATUS: Annual SV.

Lesser Kestrel
Falco naumanni (Falco cenchris). 29-32cm.
DISTRIBUTION: Southern Palearctic. Winters mainly in sub-Saharan Africa; some over-winter in southern Europe and north-western Africa. HABITAT: Predominantly in open areas, with short vegetation and often bare patches. In winter also in savannas, steppe, thorn-bush vegetation, open grasslands or farmlands. FOOD: Chiefly insects. STATUS: Irregular SV. ***Global Conservation Concern***.

Kestrel
Falco tinnunculus. 29-32cm.
DISTRIBUTION: Eurasia, Africa and southern Asia. Mainly migratory in north and east; partially migratory, dispersive or resident elsewhere. HABITAT: Open country including plains, heathlands, grasslands, wetlands with low vegetation, forest fringes, farmlands, savannas, urban areas and other suitable situations. FOOD: Chiefly small mammals, also birds and insects. STATUS: Widespread RB, also MB, PV and WV. [Common Kestrel]

———————— PLATE 39 ————————

Cormorant (Common Cormorant)
Phalacrocorax carbo. 80-100cm.
DISTRIBUTION: Nearly cosmopolitan, though not South America. Migratory, partially migratory and dispersive. HABITAT: Almost any open waters including lakes, rivers, marshes, floodlands, and coastal bays, lagoons and estuaries; nests on cliff ledges, rocks, islets, trees,

reedbeds, swamps. FOOD: Normally, entirely fish. STATUS: Common and widespread RB and MB, and some PV and WV. [Great Cormorant, does not include the White-breasted cormorant P.c.lucidus from Africa, which is kept as a separate species]

Shag (Shag or Green Cormorant)
Phalacrocorax aristotelis (Phalacrocorax graculus). 65-80cm.
DISTRIBUTION: Western Palearctic. Resident and dispersive. HABITAT: Essentially marine, especially along rocky coastlines or island groups and usually with access to sheltered inshore feeding grounds. FOOD: Almost entirely fish. STATUS: RB. [European Shag]

Northern Gannet (Gannet)
Morus bassanus (Sula bassana). 87-100cm.
DISTRIBUTION: Coastal cliffs or open islands of the northern Atlantic ocean. Dispersive or partially migratory, moving southwards as far as western Africa and Gulf of Mexico. HABITAT: Isolated stacks or small uninhabited islands for breeding, otherwise forages at sea, though rarely over deep ocean. FOOD: Chiefly fish. STATUS: MB, RB (increasing) and PV.

———————— PLATE 40 ————————

Grey Heron (Common Heron)
Ardea cinerea. 90-98cm.
DISTRIBUTION: Palearctic, southern Asia and Indonesia, and Africa. Migratory, partially migratory and dispersive; wintering to western and southern Europe east across southern Asia to Philippines, and through Africa to southern Africa. HABITAT: Prefers shallow, fresh waters, standing or flowing; also often on grasslands and other open ground. FOOD: Chiefly fish, amphibians, small mammals, insects and reptiles. STATUS: Widespread RB, and some WV.

Purple Heron
Ardea purpurea. 78-90cm.
DISTRIBUTION: Southern and eastern Eurasia, southern Asia and Malayan Archipelagos, sub-Saharan Africa. Migratory and dispersive; winters mainly to sub-Saharan Africa, and in east in southern Asia and southern Indonesia. HABITAT: Usually freshwater marshes or shallow waters with reedbeds, also mangroves; outside breeding season often on open river banks, seashores, sandspits, grasslands. FOOD: Chiefly fish and insects. STATUS: Annual and increasing PV.

Great White Egret
Ardea alba. 85-102cm.
DISTRIBUTION: Nearly cosmopolitan. Migratory, partially migratory and dispersive, wintering from Mediterranean region, south-eastern Europe, southern Asia, Philippines south through Africa, Australasian region and Americas. HABITAT: Wetlands; marshes, swamps, mangroves, reedbeds, lakes, rivers. FOOD: Chiefly fish, insects and small mammals. STATUS: SV. [Great Egret]

Little Egret
Egretta garzetta (Ardea garzetta). 55-65cm.
DISTRIBUTION: Old World. Migratory and sedentary; wintering from southern Europe and Mediterranean region east to southern and south-eastern Asia, and western Micronesia, south thoughout Africa and Australasian region to New Zealand. HABITAT: Margins of water bodies; lakes, rivers, estuaries and coastal waters, floodlands and dry fields. FOOD: Chiefly insects and small vertebrates. STATUS: Regular and annual PV.

Cattle Egret (Buff-backed Heron)
Bubulcus ibis (Ardea bubulcus). 48-53cm.
DISTRIBUTION: Marked extension of world range in recent years and now nearly cosmopolitan. Migratory and dispersive. HABITAT: Wet, and dry situations where often associated with grazing mammals. Avoids

coastal and marine habitats, cool or deep waters, mountains and extensive unvegetated areas. FOOD: Chiefly insects. STATUS: Irregular SV.

———————— PLATE 41 ————————

Squacco Heron
Ardeola ralloides (Ardea ralloides). 44-47cm.
DISTRIBUTION: Scattered across southern Palearctic and in Afrotropics and north-west Morocco. Eurasian birds winter mainly in the northern tropics of Africa. HABITAT: Nesting in mixed colonies, generally near water in dense trees, bushes or reeds. FOOD: Chiefly amphibians, fresh-water fish, and insects. STATUS: Irregular SV.

Night Heron
Nycticorax nycticorax (Nycticorax griseus). 58-65cm.
DISTRIBUTION: Southern Palearctic, southern and eastern Asia and Malayan Archipelagos; western, eastern and southern Africa; Americas. Migratory and dispersive; European populations winter in tropical Africa. HABITAT: Breeds mostly in trees near water, also in thickets of emergent vegetation and reedbeds. Feeds in ricefields, marshes, swamps, lagoons, mangroves, and other wetlands. FOOD: Chiefly amphibians, fish and insects. STATUS: Regular SV. [Black-crowned Night Heron]

Little Bittern
Ixobrychus minutus (Ardetta minuta). 33-38cm.
DISTRIBUTION: Palearctic, Afrotropics and Australasia. European populations winter principally in eastern Africa south to South Africa. HABITAT: Reedbeds and other dense vegetation along rivers, fringes of lakes, marshes, swamps and ponds. STATUS: CB (first time proven 1984) and SV, mainly April to October.

Bittern
Botaurus stellaris. 70-80cm.
DISTRIBUTION: Palearctic and an isolated population in southern Africa. In Europe northern and eastern populations are migratory moving south in winter, western populations more sedentary. HABITAT: Marshes, reedbeds, lagoons. FOOD: Mainly fish, amphibians and aquatic invertebrates. STATUS: RB and WV; long-term decline and only 22 males observed in 1996. *UK Red Listed.* [Great Bittern]

American Bittern
Botaurus lentiginosus. 60-85cm.
DISTRIBUTION: Breeds North America. Winters from south-western British Columbia to southern USA and Central America. HABITAT: Marshes, reedbeds. FOOD: Invertebrates, fish, amphibians, reptiles, and small rodents. STATUS: Irregular SV, mostly late autumn.

Glossy Ibis
Plegadis falcinellus. 55-65cm.
DISTRIBUTION: Discontinuously in southern Paleartcic and southern Asia, Malayan Archipelagos, western, eastern and southern African region, Australia and eastern and south-eastern USA to northern Venezuela. Migratory and dispersive; European birds winter eastern Mediterranean or Africa. HABITAT: Marshes, swamps, lagoons, lakes, irrigated farmlands and ricefields. FOOD: Invertebrates, mainly insects and their larvae, also small amphibians and fish. STATUS: Irregular SV.

———————— PLATE 42 ————————

White Stork
Ciconia ciconia (Ciconia alba). 100-115cm.
DISTRIBUTION: Western and central Palearctic, south-western and central Asia and few in eastern and southern Africa. Winters south in Afrotropics and east to India, Thailand and China. HABITAT: Dry or wet grasslands, farmlands, steppes, savannas, marshes, ricefields, around human habitation. FOOD: Invertebrates, especially insects, also amphibians, reptiles, small mammals and other aquatic organisms. STATUS: Regular SV.

Black Stork
Ciconia nigra. 95-100cm.
DISTRIBUTION: Central and southern Eurasia; southern Africa. Northern populations winter south to sub-Saharan Africa, central India and south-eastern Asia. HABITAT: In or near lowland moist forests and mixed and dry coniferous woods, swampy meadows, lakes, streams and ponds. FOOD: Chiefly fish; also insects, amphibians and to lesser extent small mammals, passerine nestlings, reptiles, and crustaceans. STATUS: Irregular SV.

Spoonbill
Platalea leucorodia. 80-90cm.
DISTRIBUTION: Locally in southern and central Palearctic and southern Asia. Northern populations winter south to Mediterranean region, northern tropics of Africa, north-eastern Africa, and southern Asia. HABITAT: Shallow wetlands typically, deltas, mudflats, swamps, lakes, lagoons. FOOD: Chiefly invertebrates, especially insects, and small fish. STATUS: FB, PV and WV, mainly south-east England. [Eurasian Spoonbill]

Greater Flamingo (Flamingo)
Phoenicopterus ruber ruber (Phoenicopterus roseus). 125-145cm.
DISTRIBUTION: Locally in southern Palearctic, south-western Asia and western, eastern and southern Africa. Sedentary, dispersive and migratory; related to season and hydrological factors. HABITAT: Shallow brackish and saltwater lagoons, and at times in freshwater marshes and ricefields. FOOD: Chiefly small aquatic invertebrates, their eggs and larvae. STATUS: Rarely recorded in Britain and as most are likely to be escapes, included only in D1 category of British-Irish List.

———————— PLATE 43 ————————

Greylag Goose (Grey-Lag Goose)
Anser anser (Anser cinereus). 75-90cm.
DISTRIBUTION: Northern and central Eurasia. Winters south to north-western Africa, Asia Minor, India, Burma and Indochina. HABITAT: Open fresh waters with dense fringe vegetation, with access to grazing pastures, meadows and wetlands; stubble, crops, saltmarshes. FOOD: Plant materials, above and below ground. STATUS: RB and IB (ca.13,000 feral breeding pairs, 1991) and WV.

White-fronted Goose
Anser albifrons. 65-78cm.
DISTRIBUTION: Northern Eurasia, northern North America and western Greenland. Winters south to Mediterranean region, Asia Minor, India, eastern China and southern USA and Mexico. HABITAT: Shrubby tundra near water, pastures and meadows, arable fields, grasslands and wetlands. FOOD: Plant materials, chiefly leaves, stems, stolons, rhizomes, tubers and seeds. STATUS: WV. [Greater White-fronted Goose]

Bean Goose
Anser fabalis (Anser segetum). 66-84cm.
DISTRIBUTION: Northern and central Eurasia. Winters in western and central Europe, Iran, China and Japan. HABITAT: Breeds wet low tundra, lakes, ponds, meadows and dense coniferous forests or birch scrub; on migration and in winter, marshes, floodlands, rivers and coastal shallows, arable fields. FOOD: grasses, cereal grains and other crops. STATUS: WV.

Pink-footed Goose
Anser brachyrhynchus. 60-75cm.
DISTRIBUTION: Northwestern Palearctic. Winters north-western Europe. HABITAT: Mainly on tundra lakes, ponds, sluggish rivers, swamps, wet meadows. In winter roosts on estuary flats or lakes and moves to

arable land. FOOD: Plant materials above and below ground. STATUS: WV; steady increase in recent years.

————— PLATE 44 —————

Snow Goose
Anser caerulescens (Chen hyperboreus). 65-80cm.
DISTRIBUTION: North-eastern Siberia and northern North America. Winters coastal North America to Mexico, eastern China and Japan. HABITAT: Open tundra; in winter quarters, grasslands and wetlands, often coastal. FOOD: Plant materials. STATUS: Regular SV but escapes probably account for many records.

Red-breasted Goose
Branta ruficollis (Bernicla ruficollis). 53-56cm.
DISTRIBUTION: North-western Siberia on Taimyr, Gydan and Yamal peninsulas. Winters mainly on Black Sea coasts of Romania and Bulgaria. HABITAT: Tundra or open parts of northern shrub tundra. During winter feed on agriculture lands, particularly grasslands and cereal fields. FOOD: Grazes, chiefly on green parts of plants. STATUS: Occasional SV. ***Global Conservation Concern.***

Barnacle Goose (Bernacle Goose)
Branta leucopsis (Bernicla leucopsis). 58-70cm.
DISTRIBUTION: Northern Palearctic. Winters south to Mediterranean region. HABITAT: Arctic islets or steep cliffs inland. In winter mainly on cultivated grasslands near its roosting areas and in spring on salt-marshes and arable fields. FOOD: Plant materials, chiefly grasses and other herbaceous species. STATUS: WV in Scotland (increasing) and Ireland.

Brent Goose
Branta bernicla (Bernicla brenta). 56-61cm.
DISTRIBUTION: North-western Palearctic and northern North America; Migratory, wintering to the south. HABITAT: Tundra; in autumn and winter primarily inter-tidal mudflats, in spring salt-marshes; also grasslands and winter cereal fields near coasts. FOOD: Plant materials; chiefly Zostera and green algae, salt-marsh species, grasses, mosses, lichens. STATUS: WV (*B.b.brota* and *B.b.bernicla*), in increasing numbers, also SV (*B.b.nigricans*).

————— PLATE 45 —————

Whooper Swan
Cygnus cygnus (Cygnus musicus). 145-160cm.
DISTRIBUTION: Northern and central Palearctic. Winters south to north-western Europe or to south-eastern Europe across to the Caspian and Aral Seas. HABITAT: Mainly swampy lakes and river deltas. Winters on coastal and inland wetlands and floodlands, also arable farmlands. FOOD: Chiefly aquatic vegetation, also grasses, grain and crop vegetables. STATUS: CB, some probably feral, and WV.

Bewick's Swan and Whistling Swan
Cygnus columbianus (Cygnus bewicki). 115-127cm.
DISTRIBUTION: Northern Eurasia and northern North America. Winters in north-western Europe and eastern Asia, and in North America. HABITAT: Sedge grass and moss-lichen tundra with small lakes. In winter uses lakes, marshes, flooded pastures and arable fields. FOOD: Plant materials, mainly leaves, stems, roots, rhizomes and tubers, especially aquatic species and grasses. STATUS: WV (*C.c.bewickii*) and increasing, and SV (*C.c.columbianus*). [Tundra Swan]

Mute Swan
Cygnus olor. 145-160cm.
DISTRIBUTION: Northern and central Eurasia. Populations sedentary, partially migratory or wholly migratory; moving mainly to coasts from frozen lakes. HABITAT: Lakes, ponds, marshes, rivers, deltas; in west

largely conditioned to relatively close proximity to man and frequently dependent on artificial habitats and food. FOOD: Aquatic vegetation, emergent plants and seeds, grasses and herbaceous plants. STATUS: RB.

————— PLATE 46 —————

Common Shelduck
Tadorna tadorna (Tadorna cornuta). 58-67cm.
DISTRIBUTION: Southern and western Palearctic. Winters south to northern Africa, northern India, Burma and southern China. HABITAT: In north-western Europe, sandy and muddy coasts and estuaries; in central Asia, inland salt lakes and marshes. FOOD: Chiefly invertebrates, especially molluscs, insects and crustaceans. STATUS: MB, RB and WV.

Ruddy Shelduck
Tadorna ferruginea (Tadorna casarca). 61-67cm.
DISTRIBUTION: Palearctic; north-western Africa, south-eastern Europe and central Asia. Winters south to Nile valley, southern India, and southern Asia. HABITAT: Shallow, sparsely vegetated marshes and lakes often in semi-arid regions; brackish, shallow water with vegetation-free areas for feeding preferred. FOOD: Omnivorous. STATUS: Regular SV but all recent records considered to be of captive origin.

Mallard
Anas platyrhynchos (Anas boscas). 50-65cm.
DISTRIBUTION: Palearctic and Nearctic. Sedentary and migratory; winters south to north Africa, India, south-eastern China, Mexico and the Antilles. Introduced Australia and New Zealand; widely domesticated. HABITAT: Adapts to wide range of habitats, toleration of people, and exploitation of artificial foods; essentially a bird of still and shallow, fresh-, brackish-, and salt-water. FOOD: Omnivorous and opportunistic. STATUS: Common and widespread, RB and WV.

Gadwall
Anas strepera. 46-56cm.
DISTRIBUTION: Palearctic and North America. Migratory and sedentary. Winters in south of breeding range and to North Africa, Nile valley, India, Burma, south-eastern China, southern Mexico, Florida and Gulf coast. HABITAT: Prefers shallow, still or slow-moving, open waters with fringe vegetation and islands. In winter large wetlands, lakes, deltas, estuaries and lagoons. FOOD: Chiefly vegetative parts of emergent and submergent plants. STATUS: IB, RB, MB and WV

————— PLATE 47 —————

Shoveler
Anas clypeata (Spatula clypeata). 44-52cm.
DISTRIBUTION: Eurasia and North America. Winters south to northern, western, north-central and eastern Africa (rarely southern), India, southern Asia to Philippines, Polynesia and northern South America. HABITAT: Shallow, permanent, often small waters, fringed by dense reeds or other emergent vegetation; also pastures, grasslands, rice-fields, rivers and brackish marshes. FOOD: Omnivorous but especially planktonic organisms filtered from surface. STATUS: MB, PV and WV. [Northern Shoveler]

Pintail
Anas acuta (Dafila acuta). 51-66cm.
DISTRIBUTION: Palearctic and North America. Winters south to northern Africa and northern Afrotropics, Arabia, Indian Ocean, Philippines, Hawaiian Islands, Micronesia, and northern South America. HABITAT: Shallow waters of open grasslands or prairies. In winter, prefers sheltered coastal areas, estuaries, floodlands and nearby inland waters; also farmlands and stubble. FOOD: Omnivorous. STATUS: RB or MB (8-42, 1989-93), common WV. [Northern Pintail]

Teal
Anas crecca (Nettion crecca). 34-38cm.
DISTRIBUTION: Northern and central Eurasia, western Alaska and North America. Winters south to northern and tropical Africa, southern Asia, Philippines, Micronesia, Hawaiian Islands, northern central America and West Indies. HABITAT: Normally small, densely fringed waterbodies within larger wetland systems. In winter and on passage shallow tidal coasts, estuaries, salt-marshes, reservoirs. FOOD: Omnivorous with seeds predominating in winter. STATUS: RB and common WV. [Common Teal]

Green-winged Teal (American Green-winged Teal *Anas carolinense*): now considered to be a subspecies, *Anas crecca carolinensis*, which is a fairly regular SV.

Blue-winged Teal (American Blue-winged Teal)
Anas discors. 37-41cm.
DISTRIBUTION: North America and eastern Hawaiian Islands. Winters from southern USA south to Argentina. HABITAT: Shallow lake margins, reedbeds, ponds, lagoons, streams and marshes. FOOD: Omnivorous, but especially seeds. STATUS: Regular SV.

PLATE 48

Garganey
Anas querquedula (Querquedula circia). 37-41cm.
DISTRIBUTION: Eurasia. Totally migratory; winters to south of breeding range in subtropical and tropical Africa, India and southern Asia to the Philippines. HABITAT: Favours sheltered and shallow fresh waters merging into grasslands, floodlands or other wetlands with floating or emergent vegetation. FOOD: Omnivorous. STATUS: MB, small numbers, and PV.

Wigeon
Anas penelope (Mareca penelope). 45-51cm.
DISTRIBUTION: Northern and central Eurasia. Winters in western and southern Europe, south to northern, western and eastern Africa, Arabia and southern Asia to the Philippines. HABITAT: Open waters with submerged or floating vegetation, using nesting cover in wooded areas and on open moors; in winter and on migration sheltered, coastal waters with marshes or tidal flats, also flooded grasslands and inland lakes. FOOD: Chiefly vegetation and seeds. STATUS: RB and common WV. [Eurasian Wigeon]

American Wigeon
Anas americana (Mareca americana). 45-56cm.
DISTRIBUTION: Northern and central North America. Winters mainly south of breeding range, principally coastal areas of Atlantic and Neotropics south to Colombia. HABITAT: Shallow, sheltered inshore waters, estuaries and deltas, as well as freshwater lakes, pools and rivers, grasslands and crops. FOOD: Almost entirely vegetation. STATUS: SV, with some of captive origin.

Red-crested Pochard
Netta rufina. 53-57cm.
DISTRIBUTION: Locally in southern Palearctic. Winters in south of breeding range around the Mediterranean, and in Iraq, Iran, India and Burma, and southern China. HABITAT: Islets in river deltas, lowland lakes, estuaries and other coastal areas with reedbeds. Winters in coastal or inland waters, open or fringed with reedbeds. FOOD: Chiefly aquatic plants. STATUS: CB and PV but many recent records considered to be of captive origin.

Pochard
Aythya ferina (Fuligula ferina). 42-49cm.
DISTRIBUTION: Palearctic. Winters within breeding range and south to tropical Africa, India, south-eastern Asia. HABITAT: Open waters with

fringing vegetation and overgrown islets; also in winter and on migration brackish areas and estuaries. FOOD: Omnivorous bottom feeders. STATUS: MB or RB, common PV and WV. [Common Pochard]

PLATE 49

Ferruginous Duck
Aythya nyroca (Fuligula nyroca). 38-42cm.
DISTRIBUTION: Central and south-western Palearctic. Winters southern part of breeding range and south to northern, western and eastern Africa, India, south-eastern Asia, and eastern China. HABITAT: Shallow, plant-fringed waters with emergent vegetation and diverse submergent plants. Winters mainly in coastal or large inland fresh water and brackish water bodies. FOOD: Omnivorous, mainly plant materials. STATUS: Rare though regular PV. ***Global Conservation Concern***.

Tufted Duck
Aythya fuligula (Fuligula cristata). 40-47cm.
DISTRIBUTION: Eurasia. Winters in south of breeding range and beyond as far as Mediterranean region, northern and eastern Africa, Arabia, India, south-eastern Asia, eastern China and Philippines. HABITAT: Open fresh waters, natural and man-made; also in winter sheltered sea-coasts, rivers and tidal estuaries. FOOD: Omnivorous. STATUS: RB, PV and WV.

Greater Scaup (Scaup-duck)
Aythya marila (Fuligula marila). 42-51cm.
DISTRIBUTION: Northern Eurasia and northern North America. Winters, mainly on coasts, south to Mediterranean Sea, Persian Gulf, east China, Philippines, and south to Baja California and southern USA. HABITAT: Tundra lakes and ponds, on migration and in winter mainly coastal areas. FOOD: Omnivorous though molluscs predominate in wintering areas. STATUS: CB (Scotland), common PV and WV.

Goldeneye
Bucephala clangula (Clangula glaucion). 42-53cm.
DISTRIBUTION: Northern and central Eurasia and northern and north-central North America. Winters south to Mediterranean Sea, Iran, south-eastern China, Japan and to California, Mexico, Gulf coast and Florida. HABITAT: Hole nester in tall forest growth close to lakes, pools or rivers with open water. In winter fresh and salt water, especially reservoirs, estuaries, marine bays, shallow coasts and sewage outfalls. FOOD: Chiefly animal with molluscs, crustaceans and insect larvae predominating. STATUS: RB (small numbers, mostly in Scotland), common PV and WV. [Common Goldeneye]

Bufflehead (Buffle-headed Duck)
Bucephala albeola (Clangula albeola). 32-39cm.
DISTRIBUTION: Northern Nearctic. Winters south to southern USA, central Mexico and Greater Antilles. HABITAT: Lakes, ponds in wooded areas; also on migration and in winter, sea-coasts and inland waters. FOOD: Chiefly invertebrates, especially molluscs. STATUS: SV.

Long-tailed Duck
Clangula hyemalis (Harelda glacialis). 40-47cm.
DISTRIBUTION: Northern Palearctic and northern North America. Winters mainly off-shore within its breeding range and to the south reaching southern North Sea and the Baltic, eastern China and Japan, and southern USA. HABITAT: Tundra, especially of high arctic, on islands and skerries, also inland in vegetation with water areas. Winters predominantly off coasts, occasionally inland waters. FOOD: Chiefly animal, especially crustaceans and molluscs. STATUS: CB and WV.

———— PLATE 50 ————

Harlequin Duck
Histrionicus histrionicus (Cosmonetta histrionica). 38-45cm.
DISTRIBUTION: Western Palearctic (Iceland) and western and north-eastern North America. Winters within or just south of breeding range. HABITAT: Tundra, high altitude streams, lake outlets and spring-fed rivers. Winters on rocky seashores. FOOD: Animal, especially crustaceans and molluscs in winter; insect adults and larvae in spring and summer. STATUS: SV.

Eider
Somateria mollissima. 50-71cm.
DISTRIBUTION: Northern Palearctic, Arctic and northern North America. Partially migratory and dispersive, with some movement south in winter. HABITAT: Essentially coastal and marine, breeding on islands, rocky shores and by sand-flats and saltings, estuaries and lakes. Wintering mainly on sea-coasts. FOOD: Chiefly molluscs, also crustaceans and echinoderms. STATUS: RB and WV, also SV (*S.m. borealis*; dead on tideline). [Common Eider]

King Eider
Somateria spectablis. 47-63cm.
DISTRIBUTION: Arctic Eurasia and North America. Migratory, though some only partially, wintering south to Norway, Iceland, Kamchatka, Aleutians, and along coasts of North America. HABITAT: Inland fresh-water pools, lagoons and rivers in tundra and in winter, open waters of Arctic Ocean and coastlines. FOOD: Chiefly molluscs, crustaceans and echinoderms. STATUS: Regular SV.

———— PLATE 51 ————

Steller's Eider
Polysticta stelleri (Somateria stelleri). 43-47cm.
DISTRIBUTION: Arctic coast of Alaska and eastern Siberia. Most winter in northern Pacific but main areas for European wintering and non-breeding birds are northern Norway and the Murmansk coast. HABITAT: Nests inland among pools on flat coastal belt within tundra zone. Winters mainly along sea-coasts. FOOD: Molluscs and crustaceans, also other invertebrates and fish. STATUS: SV. **Global Conservation Concern**.

Common Scoter
Melanitta nigra (Oedemia nigra). 44-54cm.
DISTRIBUTION: Northern Eurasia, eastern Siberia and north-western Alaska, locally in central and eastern Canada. Winters south to Moroccan Atlantic coast, Baltic, Black, Caspian and Bering Seas, and North Pacific and western North America to California. HABITAT: Inland in tundra vegetation or dwarf heath, on islets, river banks; outside breeding period predominantly marine, in shallow, inshore waters. FOOD: Mainly molluscs. STATUS: RB or MB (small numbers), common PV and WV, SV (*M.n.americana*). **UK Red Listed**. [Black Scoter]

Velvet Scoter
Melanitta fusca (Oedemia fusca). 51-58cm.
DISTRIBUTION: Northern and south-central Eurasia, central and south-western Siberia, and northern North America. Winters south to Mediterranean, Black and Caspian Seas, inland American Great Lakes and American coast to south Carolina, and Pacific coasts to California and eastern China and Japan. HABITAT: In taiga zones and wooded tundra near water, and in alpine areas and coastal zones on wooded islands and skerries. Winters primarily along exposed shores or offshore. FOOD: Molluscs, crustaceans, echinoderms and annelids, inland chiefly insects, fish and some plant material. STATUS: PV and WV. [White-winged Scoter]

Surf Scoter
Melanitta perspicillata (Oedemia perspicillata) 45-56cm.
DISTRIBUTION: Northern North America. Winters coasts of North America and on Great Lakes. HABITAT: Bogs, lake or pond margins, within or beyond tree limit. Outside breeding period mainly in inshore marine waters and large lakes. FOOD: Primarily molluscs. STATUS: Rare PV and WV, usually amongst flocks of Common and Velvet Scoters.

———— PLATE 52 ————

Goosander
Mergus merganser. 58-66cm.
DISTRIBUTION: Northern and south-central Eurasia, western and northern North America. Winters south to Mediterranean and Black Sea, Iran, northern India, east China, southern USA and Mexico. HABITAT: Hole nester, mainly in trees or other suitable cavities, near rivers, lakes. In winter moves to large open waters, including marine inlets. FOOD: Primarily fish. STATUS: RB and WV. [Common Merganser]

Red-breasted Merganser
Mergus serrator. 52-58cm.
DISTRIBUTION: Northern and south-central Palearctic, and northern and north-eastern North America. Winters south to Mediterranean, Black and Caspian Seas, southern Russia, eastern China, Japan, southern USA and northern Mexico. HABITAT: Sheltered, shallow salt water bays, inlets or estuaries, also lakes, islands and rivers. Wintering mainly in coastal and estuarine areas; reservoirs and barrages visited on passage. FOOD: Primarily fish. STATUS: RB and WV.

Smew
Mergellus albellus (Mergus albellus). 38-44cm.
DISTRIBUTION: Northern Eurasia. Winters south to British Isles, France, around Mediterranean and Black Seas, Persian Gulf, northern India, east China and Japan. HABITAT: Tree-hole nester in coniferous and mixed forests, near fresh water lakes, ponds. In winter, mainly fresh waters or sheltered, shallow bays, estuaries and inlets. FOOD: In winter and spring chiefly fish, at other times mainly insects. STATUS: WV.

Hooded Merganser
Lophodytes cucullatus (Mergus cucullatus). 42-50cm.
DISTRIBUTION: Western and eastern North America. Winters southern USA and Mexico along Pacific and Atlantic coasts. HABITAT: Inland waters, usually small, standing, or gently flowing, surrounded by trees (essential for tree-hole nesting). In winter moves to rivers and brackish coastal areas. FOOD: Primarily aquatic insects, fish and crustaceans. STATUS: SV.

———— PLATE 53 ————

Woodpigeon (Wood-Pigeon)
Columba palumbus. 40-42cm.
DISTRIBUTION: Western Palearctic. Largely residential, partially migratory or migratory; wintering southwards in or beyond breeding range. HABITAT: Highly adaptable to changing land-use or climate. Woodlands, farmlands, towns. FOOD: Chiefly plant material, occasionally invertebrates. STATUS: RB and WV: common, widespread and increasing. [Common Wood Pigeon]

Stock Dove (Stock-Dove)
Columba oenas. 32-34cm.
DISTRIBUTION: Western Palearctic. Residential, partially migratory to migratory; northern populations wintering south to Mediterranean area, including north-western and north-eastern Africa, northern Arabia and southern Iran. HABITAT: Open woodlands, parks, farmlands, also when nesting, cliffs, ruins. FOOD: Chiefly plant material, occasionally invertebrates. STATUS: RB, PV and WV. [Stock Pigeon]

Rock Dove (Rock-Dove)
Columba livia. 31-34cm.
Distribution: Cosmopolitan; probably originally native of Palearctic but range obscure because of long history of domestication. Habitat: Natural habitat linked with nest-site on rock-faces, particularly coastal. Feral form strongly attached to human settlements. Food: Chiefly seeds and invertebrates, feral birds also take wide variety of artificial foods. Status: RB plus abundant feral population of domestic origin. [Rock Pigeon]

Turtle Dove (Turtle-Dove)
Streptopelia turtur (Turtur communis). 26-28.
Distribution: Central and south-western Palearctic. Winters in northern tropical Africa. Habitat: Hedges, open woodlands, forest edges, scrublands, gardens, plains, young plantations, farmlands and in winter quarters, open savannas. Food: Chiefly seeds and fruits of weeds and cereals. Status: MB and PV. Considerable decline since ca.1970s. *UK Red Listed.* [European Turtle Dove]

Pallas's Sandgrouse (Pallas's Sand-Grouse)
Syrrhaptes paradoxus 30-41cm.
Distribution: Central Asia. Mainly sedentary or partially migratory southwards in and beyond breeding range; also irregularly eruptive. Habitat: Arid open plains and uplands. Food: Chiefly seeds, also green shoots. Status: CB (1888 and 1889) and SV.

———————— Plate 54 ————————

Capercaillie
Tetrao urogallus. 60-87cm.
Distribution: Northern and north-central Eurasia. Mainly resident. Habitat: Chiefly mature coniferous forests; also locally in mixed stands and deciduous woodlands. Food: Plant materials, especially Pine Pinus needles, also, outside winter, leaves, stems and berries. Status: FB (extinct ca.1770) and IB (re-introduced Scotland 1837). *UK Red Listed.* [Western Capercaillie]

———————— Plate 55 ————————

Black Grouse
Tetrao tetrix. 40-55cm.
Distribution: Northern Eurasia. Mainly sedentary. Habitat: In areas transitional between forest or woodland and open heath, marginal cultivation, bogs and fens, or steppes. Trees, in scattered groups, essential. Food: Chiefly plant material, especially buds, shoots, leaves, catkins, and berries. Status: RB, declined throughout most of range. *UK Red Listed.*

Red Grouse
Lagopus lagopus (Lagopus scoticus). 37-42cm.
Distribution: Northern Palearctic and northern North America. Resident, except Russian tundra where apparently partially migratory. Habitat: Tundra, moors, heaths, bogs, also open wetlands and dunelands; after breeding season some races move into wooded tundra and woodlands with open clearings. Food: Chiefly plant material, also, at times in some areas, invertebrates. Status: RB; annual numbers of the British and Irish race L.l.scoticus, once considered to be a separate species, fluctuate considerably. [Willow Ptarmigan]

———————— Plate 56 ————————

Ptarmigan
Lagopus mutus. 34-36cm.
Distribution: Northern Palearctic and northern North America. Basically resident though some movements, especially in years of high population levels, occur in arctic latitudes. Habitat: Open rocky or stony terrain interspersed with low vegetation. Food: Chiefly plant material; especially shoots, twigs, catkins, buds, leaves, bulbils, and berries. Status: RB (restricted to Scotland). [Rock Ptarmigan]

———————— Plate 57 ————————

Pheasant
Phasianus colchicus. 53-89cm.
Distribution: Indigenous only in south-central Eurasia, eastern and southern Asia, and Japan. Introduced Europe, Australia, New Zealand, Hawaiian Islands, central and southern Canada, northern USA. Habitat: Open country, farmlands, scrubby wastes, woodlands, grassy steppes, thickets, swamps. Food: Omnivorous. Status: IB, common and widespread. [Common Pheasant]

Also illustrated on this plate are the **Mongolian Pheasant, Chinese Ring-necked Pheasant** and the **Japanese Pheasant.** The first two are now considered to be merely races of the **Common Pheasant** and are named respectively *P.colchicus mongolicus* and *P.c.torquatus.* The **Japanese** or **Green Pheasant**, which is native to Japan, appears to represent an isolated stock and is sometimes considered a separate species, *P. versicolor.*

———————— Plate 58 ————————

Grey Partridge (Common Partridge)
Perdix perdix (Perdix cinerea). 29-31cm.
Distribution: Western and central Eurasia. Mainly resident. Introduced North America. Habitat: Open, low-intensity mixed farmlands, with small fields and hedges, also woodland edges, steppes, meadows. Food: Chiefly plant materials, especially leaves and seeds. Insects important in breeding season. Status: Considerable decline; RB intraspecific hybrids as a result of introductions, FB *P.p.perdix.* *UK Red Listed.*

Red-legged Partridge
Alectoris rufa (Caccabis rufa). 32-34cm.
Distribution: Southwestern Palearctic. Sedentary in natural range. Introduced British Isles, Madeira, Canaries and Azores. Habitat: Arable farming, preferably low-intensity cropping with a mixture of cultivated, fallow and uncultivated ground; also rocky mountain slopes with bare ground and low shrubs. Food: Chiefly seeds, leaves and roots. Chick survival depends on insects and grass seeds. Status: IB, and has interbred widely with released Chukar A.chukar with resultant hybrids.

Quail
Coturnix coturnix (Coturnix communis). 16-18cm.
Distribution: Palearctic, eastern and southern Africa. Migratory and winters from Mediterranean region and Arabia south to tropical Africa and north to Angola and Zaire. Habitat: Open spaces with low vegetation, especially arable lands cultivated and fallow, and natural grasslands and meadows. Food: Omnivorous, mainly seeds and invertebrates. Status: MB, numbers fluctuate. *UK Red Listed.* [Common Quail]

———————— Plate 59 ————————

Corncrake (Land-Rail)
Crex crex (Crex pratensis). 27-30cm.
Distribution: Eurasia, with fragmented distribution in western Europe and much restricted elsewhere. Migrates in autumn, especially through Egypt, to winter in sub-Saharan Africa. Habitat: Open or semi-open landscapes, mainly in meadows of tall grass, especially those annually mown, grazed or winter flooded. Food: Omnivorous;

in breeding season chiefly invertebrates and occasionally small vertebrates (fish, amphibians); in autumn and winter mainly seeds. STATUS: MB and PV. Serious decline; estimated only 489 singing males in UK (1993). *UK Red Listed*. and *Global Conservation Concern*. [Corn Crake]

Spotted Crake
Porzana porzana (Porzana maruetta). 22-24cm.
DISTRIBUTION: Western and central Eurasia. Mainly migratory, wintering in southern Europe and eastern Africa, south of the Sahara and east to India, Burma and Thailand. HABITAT: Lowland swamps and fens, edges of lakes and rivers, and upland bogs. FOOD: Omnivorous, chiefly small aquatic invertebrates and parts of aquatic plants. STATUS: CB (1-20 pairs 1989-93), scarce PV, rare WV.

Sora (Carolina Crake)
Porzana carolina. 20-23cm.
DISTRIBUTION: North America. Winters from southern USA south through Middle America and West Indies to northern South America. HABITAT: Marshes and wetlands with floating vegetation. On passage occurs on brackish coastal marshes, wild rice beds, stubble fields, brushy hillsides; in Caribbean in mangrove swamps. FOOD: Seeds and aquatic invertebrates. STATUS: SV.

Little Crake
Porzana parva. 18-20cm.
DISTRIBUTION: Western and central Eurasia. Winters from Mediterranean region and north-eastern and East Africa east to north-western India. HABITAT: Freshwater wetlands; marshes, margins of rivers and lakes, flooded woodlands. FOOD: Mainly small invertebrates and aquatic plant seeds. STATUS: SV.

Baillon's Crake
Porzana pusilla (Porzana bailloni). 17-19cm.
DISTRIBUTION: Imperfectly known; southern Palearctic, eastern and south-eastern Africa, western Indonesia and Australasian region. Northern populations winter south to Ethiopian Africa east to southern and south-eastern Asia. HABITAT: River deltas, marshlands and inland wetlands, including man-made areas. FOOD: Omnivorous; mainly aquatic insects. STATUS: FB (1858, 1889 and probably 1866), and SV.

Water Rail (Water-Rail)
Rallus aquaticus. 23-28cm.
DISTRIBUTION: Palearctic. Mainly resident in west and south, migratory elsewhere; wintering south to northern Africa and Arabia east to south-eastern Asia. HABITAT: Fresh waters, flat usually muddy ground with dense, fairly tall, aquatic vegetation. FOOD: Omnivorous. STATUS: RB, PV and WV.

Moorhen (Moor-Hen)
Gallinula chloropus. 32-35cm.
DISTRIBUTION: Nearly cosmopolitan, though not Australasian. Resident, partially migratory to migratory with northern populations moving south in winter. HABITAT: Requires access to fresh water with some plant cover, including pools, streams, ditches, lakes, rivers, marshes. FOOD: Omnivorous. STATUS: RB and WV, common and widespread. [Common Moorhen]

Coot
Fulica atra. 36-38cm.
DISTRIBUTION: Palearctic, southern Asia and Australasian region. Sedentary and partially migratory to migratory, with northern populations (except western Europe) moving west and south. HABITAT: Open waters with shallows and vegetation; lakes, barrages, reservoirs, lagoons, pools, gravel-pits, slow-moving rivers, and in winter sheltered estuaries. FOOD: Omnivorous, chiefly plant materials. STATUS: RB and WV, common and widespread. [Common Coot]

---------- PLATE 60 ----------

Great Bustard
Otis tarda. 75-105cm.
DISTRIBUTION: Palearctic but range much fragmented. Migratory in north and east, dispersive or resident elsewhere. HABITAT: Extensive, gently undulating treeless, predominantly grass, plains, and mixed landforms of arable, fallow and pasture. FOOD: Chiefly plants and invertebrates (mainly insects), occasionally small vertebrates. STATUS: FB (last bred Suffolk, 1832) and late winter SV. *Global Conservation Concern*.

---------- PLATE 61 ----------

Little Bustard
Tetrax tetrax (Otis tetrax). 40-45cm.
DISTRIBUTION: Southern Palearctic; highly fragmented populations. Resident, dispersive and migratory in different regions with northern and east populations wintering southwards. HABITAT: Grass plains or arable land of cereal, weedy fallow and pasture, where vegetation is not too dense or higher than 30cm. FOOD: Mainly plants and invertebrates, especially insects. STATUS: SV.

Houbara Bustard (Macqueen's Bustard)
Chlamydotis undulata (Otis macqueeni). 55-65cm.
DISTRIBUTION: Southern Palearctic. Migratory in east, resident or dispersive elsewhere. HABITAT: On open or shrubby, level or undulating arid plains and areas with low sand-dunes and shrubby vegetation. FOOD: Omnivorous. STATUS: SV.

Crane
Grus grus (Grus communis). 110-120cm.
DISTRIBUTION: Eurasia. Mostly migratory moving south to winter in Spain, north-western and north-eastern Africa, Middle East, southern India and southeastern Asia. HABITAT: Wet habitats including bogs, swampy clearings in pine forests, reedy wetlands, wet woodlands and at ponds in cultivated areas. In winter and on passage in fields and meadows. FOOD: Primarily plant materials, also at times animal materials. STATUS: FB, CB (3 pairs, 1995), and increasingly common PV. [Common Crane]

Stone Curlew
Burhinus oedicnemus (Oedicnemus scolopax). 40-44cm.
DISTRIBUTION: Eurasia and south-eastern Asia. Mainly migratory in northern and eastern Europe and western Siberia, but elsewhere partially migratory to resident. HABITAT: Lowland heaths, semi-natural dry grasslands, infertile agricutural grasslands, steppes on poor soil, deserts and extensive sand-dunes. FOOD: Chiefly terrestrial invertebrates and small vertebrates. STATUS: MB, small numbers. *UK Red Listed*. [Eurasian Thick-knee or Stone-Curlew]

---------- PLATE 62 ----------

Collared Pratincole (Pratincole)
Glareola pratincola. 24-27cm.
DISTRIBUTION: Southern Palearctic and locally in Africa. Where migratory winters mainly in Africa south of the Sahara. HABITAT: Steppes, semi-deserts, fallow lands with sparse or grazed vegetation, and late sown crops, normally near water; also feed over open water, ricefields, reedbeds and coastal scrubs. FOOD: Principally insects, especially beetles and grasshoppers. STATUS: SV.

Black-winged Pratincole
Glareola nordmanni (Glareola melanoptera). 24-27cm.
DISTRIBUTION: South-central Eurasia. Winters in tropical Africa. HABITAT: Saline and alkaline steppe-like areas, in river valleys, and along shores of lakes or seas. FOOD: Invertebrates, mostly insects. STATUS: SV.

Cream-coloured Courser
Cursorius cursor (Cursorius gallicus). 22-24cm.
DISTRIBUTION: North African region and south-west and central Asia. Resident and migratory; winters east to northwestern India. HABITAT: Semi-deserts, sandy-rocky plains and sand-dunes, preferably with sparse plant cover. FOOD: Mainly insects and their larvae. STATUS: SV.

Dotterel
Charadrius morinellus (Eudromias morinellus). 20-22cm.
DISTRIBUTION: Northern and east-central Eurasia, and sporadically in north-western Alaska. Migratory, wintering mainly in North Africa and Middle East. HABITAT: Open flat uplands or mountain ridges and plateaux with sparse vegetation; on passage also on heathlands, coastal marshes, lowland fields; in winter semi-deserts with marginal cultivation, shrubby stony steppes. FOOD: Chiefly invertebrates, especially insects and spiders, also some plant materials. STATUS: MB and PV. [Eurasian Dotterel Eudromias morinellus]

Caspian Plover
Charadrius asiaticus (Aegialitis asiatica). 18-20cm.
DISTRIBUTION: South-central Asia. Winters in eastern and southern Africa. HABITAT: Arid salt steppes and desert flats, with sparse vegetation and access to water; in winter, mainly inland on grasslands recently burnt or grazed low, also newly ploughed land, gravel plains, semi-arid steppes, and true deserts. FOOD: Chiefly insects. STATUS: SV.

Ringed Plover
Charadrius hiaticula (Aegialitis hiaticola) 18-20cm.
DISTRIBUTION: Northern Palearctic and western Alaska. Migratory and sedentary; winters south mainly through to southern Africa. HABITAT: Concentrates on sandy or shingle beaches and river beds, with access to suitable resting or nesting places. In winter also inland rivers, reservoirs, lakes, mudflats. FOOD: Invertebrates. STATUS: RB, MB, PV and WV.

Little Ringed Plover
Charadrius dubius (Aegialitis curonica). 14-15cm.
DISTRIBUTION: Palearctic, southern Asia, Malayan Archipelagos, New Guinea region. Northern populations mainly migratory, wintering south to about the equator in Africa and Asia, elsewhere sedentary and migratory southwards. HABITAT: Sandy, rocky or shingly shores and banks of lakes and rivers; also outside breeding season on beaches, estuaries and shallow marshes. FOOD: Chiefly insects and other small invertebrates. STATUS: MB (first bred 1938) and PV. [Little Plover]

Kentish Plover
Charadrius alexandrinus (Aegialitis cantiana). 15-17cm.
DISTRIBUTION: Locally in Palearctic, western Indonesia, locally in Americas, and Pacific coast of south-western South America. Eurasian birds winter from southern Europe and southern and eastern Asia to tropical Africa, Indonesia and Philippines. HABITAT: Primarily sea-coasts but also on inland flats by lakes, lagoons, seasonal watercourses. FOOD: Invertebrates; mainly insects (inland), crustaceans, annelids and molluscs. STATUS: FB, CB, and scarce PV.

––––––––––– PLATE 63 –––––––––––

Kildeer (Kildeer Plover)
Charadrius vociferus (Aegialitis vocifera). 23-26cm.
DISTRIBUTION: Nearctic and Neotropic. Winters from south-eastern Alaska and southern Canada south to Peru and Chile. HABITAT: Open areas inland and coastal or away from water; fields, meadows, pastures, mudflats, lakes, ponds and rivers. FOOD: Invertebrates, mainly insects, especially beetles. STATUS: SV.

Golden Plover
Pluvialis apricaria (Charadrius pluvialis). 26-29cm.
DISTRIBUTION: Northern Eurasia. Winters from western and southern

Europe and Mediterranean region east to southern Caspian. HABITAT: Coastal and riverine tundra, upland moors, peatlands, and swampy heaths; on migration and in winter, grasslands, arable land, and open ground above foreshore. FOOD: Invertebrates, especially beetles and earthworms, and some plant materials. STATUS: RB, MB, PV and WV. [Eurasian or European Golden-Plover]

Pacific Golden Plover (Asiatic Golden Plover)
Pluvialis fulva* (Charadrius dominicus). 23-26cm.
DISTRIBUTION: North-eastern Eurasia and north-western North America. Winters mainly to southern Asia to Australasia, also Pacific and East Africa. HABITAT: Tundra uplands with mostly lichen and moss; on migration short grasslands, pastures, mudflats, sandy beaches and flooded fields. FOOD: Invertebrates, chiefly insects, also berries. STATUS: SV, mostly in the autumn. *Formerly considered conspecific with American Golden Plover or Lesser Golden Plover P. dominica.

Grey Plover
Pluvialis squatarola (Squatarola helvetica). 27-30cm.
DISTRIBUTION: Northern Eurasia and northern North America. Virtually cosmopolitan in winter, range extends to coasts of South America, Africa, southern Asia and Australia. HABITAT: Lowland tundra on sparsely vegetated terrain interspersed with lakes and near rivers. On sea-coasts mainly intertidal zone on mudflats or sandy beaches. FOOD: During breeding season mainly terrestrial invertebrates, especially insects; at other times, marine worms, molluscs and crustaceans. STATUS: Common PV and WV.

Sociable Plover
Vanellus gregaria (Vanellus gregarius). 27-30cm.
DISTRIBUTION: Central Eurasia. Winters from Israel and north-eastern Africa to northwestern India. HABITAT: Dry steppes with stands of Stipa and cover of Artemsia. At other times, ploughed fields and stubbles, creek edges, burnt areas of steppes or savannas, waste lands. FOOD: Chiefly insects. STATUS: SV. ***Global Conservation Concern.***

Lapwing
Vanellus vanellus (Vanellus vulgaris). 28-31cm.
DISTRIBUTION: Palearctic. Mainly migratory, wintering from western, central and southern Europe, southern Asia and Japan south to northern Africa, India, Burma and southern China. HABITAT: Unenclosed terrain such as open fields, pastures, wet meadows, saltings, marshes and arable lands. FOOD: Chiefly ground-living invertebrates. STATUS: RB, MB, PV and WV; since 1985 considerable decline recorded on farmland. [Northern Lapwing]

––––––––––– PLATE 64 –––––––––––

Turnstone
Arenaria interpres (Strepsilas interpres). 22-24cm.
DISTRIBUTION: Palearctic and northern North America. Winters coastally from western and southern Europe south as far as South Africa, Australia, New Zealand, southern South America. HABITAT: Tundra. Outside breeding season almost entirely coastal, preferring rocky, stony or seaweed-covered shores but also on sand- or mud-flats and inland on pasture. FOOD: In breeding season, chiefly insects with some plant materials; at other times mainly insects, crustaceans and molluscs. Also scavenges. STATUS: PV and WV. [Ruddy Turnstone]

Oystercatcher
Haematopus ostralegus. 40-45cm.
DISTRIBUTION: Eurasia. Mainly migratory. Northern populations wintering south to the Mediterranean region, western and eastern Africa, Arabia, western India and south-eastern China. HABITAT: Breeds in coastal and inland areas but outside breeding season mainly keeps to coast. FOOD: Chiefly bivalve molluscs and inland, earthworms. STATUS: RB, MB, PV and WV. [Eurasian Oystercatcher]

Avocet
Recurvirostra avosetta (Recurvirostra avocetta). 42-45cm.
DISTRIBUTION: Eurasia and northern, eastern and southern Africa. Migratory in north, grading to dispersive in south. Wintering in south-western and southern Europe southwards to southern Africa, western India and southern China. HABITAT: Estuaries, shallow bays, tidal mud-flats, coastal lagoons, brackish and freshwater pools, and steppe lakes. FOOD: Chiefly invertebrates, especially insects, crustaceans and marine worms. STATUS: RB and MB (recolonised in 1940s after ca. 100 year gap). PV and WV. [Pied Avocet]

Black-winged Stilt
Himantopus himantopus (Himantopus candidus). 34-40cm.
DISTRIBUTION: Cosmopolitan south of ca. 50_N. Sedentary or, where migratory, the more northerly populations winter south within the breeding range. HABITAT: Shallow still water, also deltas, estuaries, near swamps or lagoons, lakes and rivers. FOOD: Chiefly invertebrates, especially aquatic insects. STATUS: CB (1945) and regular, mainly spring, SV.

Grey Phalarope
Phalaropus fulicarius. 20-22cm.
DISTRIBUTION: Palearctic and northern North America. Winters at sea in southern oceans south to Antarctic waters, with major wintering areas off Chile and western Africa. HABITAT: Coastal marshy tundra; pelagic in winter. FOOD: Chiefly invertebrates. STATUS: PV, mainly mid-September to November.

Red-necked Phalarope
Phalaropus lobatus (Phalaropus hyperboreus). 18-19cm.
DISTRIBUTION: Palearctic and northern north America. Winters mainly off coasts of western South America, in Arabian Sea, and among the East Indies. HABITAT: Tundra marshes and bogs; pelagic in winter but also, on migration, inland lakes, reservoirs and sewage ponds, coastal marshes. FOOD: Chiefly invertebrates. STATUS: MB, small numbers, and PV. *UK Red Listed*.

—————————— PLATE 65 ——————————

Woodcock
Scolopax rusticola (Scolopax rusticula). 33-35cm.
DISTRIBUTION: Eurasia. Winters from western and southern Europe and southern Asia south to northern Africa, southern and south-eastern Asia and Philippines. HABITAT: Mainly in woodlands with under-growth, clearings, and wet areas; in winter also in scrublands, bogs, marshes. FOOD: Invertebrates, especially earthworms, insects and lar-vae; some plant material. STATUS: RB, MB, PV and WV; declining. [Eurasian Woodcock]

Great Snipe
Gallinago media (Gallinago major). 27-29cm.
DISTRIBUTION: North-western and north-central Eurasia. Winters mainly in Afrotropical region, especially eastern part. HABITAT: Moist areas of wooded boreal tundra, flood-plains or tussock meadows, fens, moist to drier grasslands. FOOD: Mainly earthworms, molluscs, insects; also seeds. STATUS: SV, mainly eastern Britain.

Snipe (Common Snipe)
Gallinago gallinago (Gallinago coelestis). 25-27cm.
DISTRIBUTION: Eurasia, south-western Alaska and North America. Some populations almost sedentary, others migratory; North American race winters from central USA to northern South America; Eurasian races winter in Atlantic and Mediterranean Europe and in northern tropics of Africa and southern Asia. HABITAT: Mainly open fresh or brackish marshlands with tussocky vegetation; outside breeding season, also other wetlands, ricefields, sewage farms, damp farmlands. FOOD: Chiefly invertebrates. STATUS: RB, MB, PV and WV. [Common Snipe]

Jack Snipe
Lymnocryptes minimus (Gallinago gallinula). 17-19cm.
DISTRIBUTION: Northern Eurasia. Winters mainly western and southern Europe, North Africa, northern Afrotropics, Asia Minor, northern Middle East, Iran, Afghanistan and from India to Vietnam. HABITAT: Open marshlands, bogs, swamps, also outside breeding season, flooded arable fields, ricefields. FOOD: Chiefly insect adults and larvae, molluscs, worms and plant material. STATUS: PV and WV.

Broad-billed Sandpiper
Limicola falcinellus (Limicola platyrhyncha). 16-17cm.
DISTRIBUTION: Northern Eurasia. Winters from Mediterranean region, east Africa, Arabian peninsula, east through to south-east Asia, south to Australia. HABITAT: Montane or lowland bogs, inland and coastal wet-lands, including tidal mudflats, on migration and in winter. FOOD: Invertebrates, chiefly insects and crustaceans, and seeds. STATUS: SV.

Terek Sandpiper
Xenus cinereus (Terekia cinerea). 22-24cm.
DISTRIBUTION: Northern Eurasia. Winters from Persian Gulf south to South Africa, India, south-east Asia and Australia. HABITAT: Moist grass-lands with shrubs or thickets, flooded meadows, lakesides, marshes; winters mainly on coasts and estuaries. FOOD: Invertebrates, and on breeding grounds, seeds. STATUS: SV. [Tringa cinerea]

Pectoral Sandpiper
Calidris melanotus (Tringa maculata). 19-23cm.
DISTRIBUTION: Central and eastern Siberia, and northern North America. Winters southern South America. HABITAT: Tundra; outside breeding season, wet grassy areas, marshes, moist pampas, shore mud-flats. FOOD: Chiefly insects, crustaceans, earthworms, and some plant material. STATUS: Regular PV, mainly autumn.

Baird's Sandpiper
Calidris bairdii (Tringa bairdi). 14-16cm.
DISTRIBUTION: North-eastern Siberia and northern North America. Winters in west-central and southern South America. HABITAT: Dry coastal and alpine tundra; essentially an inland species on migration in winter, preferring margins of wetlands or grasslands. FOOD: Invertebrates, especially in the breeding season, insects larvae and spiders. STATUS: Regular SV.

—————————— PLATE 66 ——————————

White-rumped Sandpiper (Bonaparte's Sandpiper)
Calidris fuscicollis (Tringa fuscicollis). 15-18cm.
DISTRIBUTION: Northern North America. Winters mainly in eastern and south-eastern South America. HABITAT: Mossy or grassy tundra; on migration and in winter wetland areas, inland and coastal, including mudflats, coastal lagoons, marshes, lakes, wet grasslands and fields. FOOD: Chiefly invertebrates, and some plant seeds. STATUS: Regular SV.

Dunlin
Calidris alpina (Tringa alpina). 16-20cm.
DISTRIBUTION: Northern Palearctic and northern North America. Winters from western and southern Europe, southern Asia and Japan south to equatorial Africa, India and Taiwan, Hawaiian Islands, and coasts of North America to Mexico. HABITAT: Upland moorlands, wet coastal grasslands and salt-marshes to high arctic tundra; non-breeding habitats include coastal mudflats, estuaries, and inland muddy sites. FOOD: Chiefly invertebrates. STATUS: MB, PV and WV. Common and widespread but some decline in recent years.

Little Stint
Calidris minuta (Tringa minuta). 12-14cm.
DISTRIBUTION: Northern Eurasia. Winters mainly in Africa, around Indian Ocean and on coasts of Indian subcontinent. HABITAT: High

119

Arctic tundra, generally on lowland drier ground but also in marshy areas. Mainly coastal when not breeding but often also uses inland wetlands, with exposed mud. FOOD: Primarily invertebrates. STATUS: Scarce, regular PV and WV.

Least Sandpiper (American Stint)
Calidris minutilla (Tringa minutilla). 11-12cm.
DISTRIBUTION: Northern North America; Winters mainly on coasts from Oregon and New Jersey south through central America, West Indies to central South America. HABITAT: Coastal and upland tundra, marshy areas in spruce forests. Outside breeding season, on sandy beaches and mudflats, also inland, often muddy wetlands. FOOD: Invertebrates, mainly crustaceans and insects. STATUS: SV, mainly autumn.

Temminck's Stint
Calidris temminckii (Tringa temmincki). 13-15cm.
DISTRIBUTION: Northern Eurasia. Most winter from Mediterranean region and northern Afrotropics across Middle East and eastwards to southern Asia and Japan. HABITAT: Tundra, grassy or mossy areas and sheltered sites on woodland fringes. Outside breeding season variety of wetland habitats, generally inland. FOOD: Principally invertebrates. STATUS: CB (1-3 pairs, 1989-93), and scarce, regular PV.

Curlew Sandpiper (Curlew-Sandpiper)
Calidris ferruginea (Tringa subarquata). 18-19cm.
DISTRIBUTION: Northern Siberia. Wintering mainly in Africa, Indian subcontinent, East Indies and Australasia. HABITAT: High arctic coastal tundra. Outside breeding season on coastal sandy beaches or mudflats, tidal estuaries, saltmarshes with pools, brackish lagoons, margins of inland lakes and rivers. FOOD: Chiefly invertebrates. STATUS: Usually scarce, mainly autumn, PV.

Purple Sandpiper
Calidris maritima (Tringa striata) 20-22cm.
DISTRIBUTION: Northern Palearctic and north-eastern North America. Migratory and partially migratory. Winters south to western Europe, and in America to Great Lakes and Florida. HABITAT: Wet coastal tundra, shingly beaches, and upland fringes of permanent snow. Essentially maritime outside breeding season, especially rocky sea-coasts. FOOD: Chiefly invertebrates, in breeding season some plant material. STATUS: CB (2 pairs, Scotland, 1989-93), PV and WV.

Knot
Calidris canutus (Tringa canutus). 23-25cm.
DISTRIBUTION: Circumpolar in high arctic latitudes. Winters from western and southern Europe, southern Asia and southern USA south to western and southern Africa, East Indies, Australasia, and southern South America. HABITAT: Moist tundra and upland glacial gravel. Outside breeding season, mainly marine inter-tidal areas. FOOD: Chiefly invertebrates, especially molluscs. On breeding grounds insects and plant material. STATUS: PV and WV. [Red Knot]

Sanderling
Calidris alba (Calidris arenaria). 20-21cm.
DISTRIBUTION: Northern Palearctic and northern North America. Winters coastal Americas and Africa, western and southern Europe, across southern Asia to Micronesia and Australia. HABITAT: High arctic tundra. After breeding season moves to tidal sandy beaches, mudflats, coral reefs, rocky shores, and occasionally inland. FOOD: Chiefly invertebrates. STATUS: PV and WV.

────────── PLATE 67 ──────────

Semipalmated Sandpiper (Semi-palmated Sandpiper)
Calidris pusilla (Tringa pusilla). 13-15cm.
DISTRIBUTION: Northern North America. Winters coastal South America and Central America. HABITAT: Wet open tundra, near pools, rivers and lakes. Outside breeding season mainly coastal, also inland, particularly on migration. FOOD: Chiefly invertebrates, aquatic and terrestrial. STATUS: SV, mainly autumn.

Ruff
Philomachus pugnax (Machetes pugnax). 26-30cm, 20-24cm.
DISTRIBUTION: Northern Eurasia and north-western Alaska. Winter range extends mainly from western Europe eastwards to India with largest numbers wintering in sub-Saharan Africa. HABITAT: Tundra wetlands, lowland marshes and wet grasslands; outside breeding season on flooded or dry grasslands, plough, ricefields, muddy margins of lakes, pools, rivers, coastal marshes. FOOD: Chiefly invertebrates, especially insects; also plant material, mainly seeds. STATUS: MB (2-24 pairs, 1989-93, PV and WV.

Buff-breasted Sandpiper
Tryngites subruficollis (Tringites rufescens). 18-20cm.
DISTRIBUTION: Northern North America. Winters central Argentina, Paraguay and Uraguay. HABITAT: Dry grassy tundra; on passage and in winter typically on short-grass areas, flodded pampas, dry open ground or muddy areas near rivers and lakes. FOOD: Chiefly invertebrates, and some seeds. STATUS: Rare and regular PV.

Upland Sandpiper (Bartram's Sandpiper)
Bartramia longicauda. 26-28cm.
DISTRIBUTION: North America. Winters to central South America. HABITAT: Chiefly prairie grasslands. On migration and in winter on pasture, alfalfa fields, rough grasslands, and short grass. FOOD: Invertebrate, mainly insects, also spiders, snails, and earthworms. STATUS: SV, usually autumn.

Common Sandpiper
Actitis hypoleucos (Totanus hypoleucus). 19-21cm.
DISTRIBUTION: Eurasia and eastern Africa. Winters chiefly in Africa south to Cape Province and across southern Asia to Melanesia and Australia. HABITAT: Rocky or shingly edges of streams and rivers, ponds, lakes; outside breeding season found in almost any freshwater site. FOOD: Chiefly invertebrates, particularly insects. STATUS: MB, PV and WV. [Tringa hypoleucos]

Spotted Sandpiper
Actitis macularia (Totanus macularius). 18-20cm.
DISTRIBUTION: North America. Winters mainly from Central America and West Indies to northern and central South America. HABITAT: Lakes, ponds, streams, farmlands; on migration and in winter sea-coasts, marshes, river banks, FOOD: Invertebrates, especially aquatic and terrestrial. STATUS: CB (attempted breeding 1975) and SV .[Tringa macularia]

Wood Sandpiper (Wood-Sandpiper)
Tringa glareola (Totanus glareola). 19-21cm.
DISTRIBUTION: Northern Eurasia and occasionally south-western Alaska. Winters mainly in Afrotropical region south of Sahara, across southern Asia to southern China, Philippines, Indonesia, and Australia. HABITAT: Damp, open parts of boreal forests or marshes with dwarf shrubs. Outside breeding season inland fresh waters and marshes. FOOD: Mainly invertebrates, particularly insects. STATUS: CB 1-5 pairs, 1989-93, Scotland) and scarce PV.

────────── PLATE 68 ──────────

Green Sandpiper
Tringa ochropus (Totanus ochropus). 21-24cm.
DISTRIBUTION: Northern Eurasia. Winters mainly Mediterranean region and Africa and across southern Asia from Turkey and Iran to eastern China and Philippines. HABITAT: Marshy areas or water margins in forests. Outside breeding season edges of lakes, pools, watercourses. FOOD: Principally invertebrates. STATUS: CB (northern Britain), PV and WV.

Solitary Sandpiper
Tringa solitaria (Totanus solitarius). 18-21cm.
DISTRIBUTION: Northern North America. Winters West Indies and Central America, but mainly inland South America to Argentina. HABITAT: Wet,open areas amongst scattered trees, often on edge of open bogs or by lakes. In winter, wooded streams, pools, bogs, river banks, creeks. FOOD: Chiefly invertebrates. STATUS: SV.

Greater Yellowlegs (Greater Yellowshank)
Tringa melanoleuca (Totanus melanoleucus). 29-31cm.
DISTRIBUTION: Northern North America. Winters mainly from southern USA, through West Indies and Central America to Tierra del Fuego. HABITAT: Tundra muskegs or bogs, usually near trees. Outside breeding season, pools, damp grassy meadows, muddy creeks and estuaries, open pampas with marshes. FOOD: Invertebrates, small fish and berries. STATUS: SV.

Redshank
Tringa totanus (Totanus calidris). 27-29cm.
DISTRIBUTION: Palearctic. Mainly migratory; winters from southern Europe, east ascross southern Asia to Philippines and south to southern Africa and Indonesia. HABITAT: Coastal and inland marshes, water meadows, moors, swampy heathlands. Outside breeding season predominantly coastal, especially on mudflats. FOOD: Invertebrates; crustaceans, molluscs, polychaete worms on estuaries, earthworms and insects inland. STATUS: Common and widespread RB, MB, PV and WV .[Common Redshank]

Spotted Redshank
Tringa erythropus (Totanus fuscus). 29-31cm.
DISTRIBUTION: Northern Eurasia. Winters from western Europe Mediterranean region and West Africa east to Vietnam and south-eastern China. HABITAT: Mainly wooded tundra and more open habitats. Outside breeding season freshwater lakeshores or brackish lagoons and sheltered muddy coasts, saltpans. FOOD: Chiefly invertebrates, especially insects, also small fish and amphibians. STATUS: PV and small number of WV.

Greenshank
Tringa nebularia (Totanus canescens). 30-33cm.
DISTRIBUTION: Northern Eurasia. Winters from British Isles and Mediterranean, but mostly south of Sahara to South Africa, Asian coasts, the Philippines, Melanesia and Australia. HABITAT: Forest clearings, moorlands and upland bogs with or without trees. Outside breeding season in a variety of open, shallow water margins, coastal and inland. FOOD: Chiefly invertebrates and small fish. STATUS: RB in Scotland, PV and WV in small numbers. [Common Greenshank]

Marsh Sandpiper
Tringa stagnatilis (Totanus stagnatilis). 22-24cm.
DISTRIBUTION: Central Eurasia. Winters mainly in Africa south of the Sahara and across southern Asia to Vietnam, Indonesia and Australia. HABITAT: Marshes, wet meadows. Outside breeding season, swampy and muddy margins of pools and lakes, floodlands, brackish lagoons, saltpans. FOOD: Invertebrates. STATUS: SV.

Short-billed Dowitcher (Red-breasted Snipe)
Limnodromus griseus (Macrorhamphus griseus). 23-25cm.
DISTRIBUTION: Northern North America. Winters from coastal southern USA, Central America to Peru and Brazil. HABITAT: Muskegs and similar open marshes and bogs. Essentially coastal in winter. FOOD: Invertebrates. STATUS: SV; identification confusion with rare but commoner vagrant, Long-billed Dowitcher *L.scopaceus.*

———————— PLATE 69 ————————

Bar-tailed Godwit
Limosa lapponica. 37-39cm.
DISTRIBUTION: Northern Eurasia and north-western North America. Winters largely on coasts of western Europe, western Africa, south-east

Asia to Australasia. HABITAT: Chiefly low-lying coastal tundra; outside breeding season mainly intertidal areas. FOOD: Invertebrates, especially insects, molluscs, crustaceans and terrestrial and marine worms. STATUS: PV and WV.

Black-tailed Godwit
Limosa limosa (Limosa belgica). 40-44cm.
DISTRIBUTION: Northern Eurasia. Winters chiefly from British Isles, Mediterranean region, Africa south of the Sahara, southern Asia to the Philippines, and Australia. HABITAT: Damp grassy moorlands, blanket-bogs, lowland wet grasslands, poorly drained farmlands. Outside breeding season mainly muddy estuaries, grasslands, floodlands, swamps, ricefields. FOOD: Chiefly invertebrates and in winter also seeds. STATUS: MB (29-53 pairs, 1989-93), PV and WV. ***UK Red-listed.***

Curlew (Common Curlew)
Numenius arquata. 50-60cm.
DISTRIBUTION: Northern Eurasia. Some resident in west of range, others winter in north-west Europe, Mediterranean region south to coasts of Africa and east through to India, southern Asia and Indonesia. HABITAT: Fens, peat-bogs, heatlands, marshes, grasslands, and farmlands. Outside breeding season mainly marine coastal areas. FOOD: Omnivorous, chiefly invertebrates. STATUS: RB, MB, PV and WV. Common and widespread. [Eurasian Curlew]

Whimbrel
Numenius phaeopus. 40-42cm.
DISTRIBUTION: Northern Eurasia and northern North America. Winters mainly along coasts of Afrotropical region, Arabia, western India, south-east Asia to Melanesia, Micronesia and Australasia; also from southern USA to Chile and Brazil. HABITAT: Lowland and upland tundra, moors and peatbogs. Outside breeding season coastal areas. FOOD: Invertebrates and plant material. STATUS: MB, PV and WV; SV (N.p.hudsonicus).

Eskimo Curlew
Numenius borealis. 29-34cm.
DISTRIBUTION: Formerly bred on tundra of Northern Canada and Alaska, migrating south along Atlantic coasts through Caribbean to winter in Uruguay, Argentina and Chile. Once abundant but by 1929 thought to be extinct. However, continues to be reported at irregular intervals. STATUS: SV, last in 1887. ***Global Conservation Concern.***

Slender-billed Curlew
Numenius tenuirostris, breeding in central Eurasia, with a total population of 50-270 individuals is of ***Global Conservation Concern.*** The three specimens from Sussex in 1910 that Thorburn mentioned, plus three others from the same year, all 'Hastings Rarities', are no longer accepted in the British/Irish List.

———————— PLATE 70 ————————

Black Tern
Chlidonias niger (Hydrochelidon nigra). 22-24cm.
DISTRIBUTION: Eurasia and North America. Winters along west coast of tropical Africa, in Americas from Panama south to Peru and east to Surinam. HABITAT: Coastal and inland lowland sites with shallow water and floating vegetation. Outside breeding season coastlines, bays, estuaries, lagoons, lakes and rivers. FOOD: When breeding, mainly insects and other invertebrates, sometimes fish and amphibians. On passage and in winter, mainly small fish, some insects and crustaceans. STATUS: FB and now CB sporadically, al✦ PV.

White-winged Black Tern
Chlidonias leucopterus (Hydrochelidon leucoptera). 20-23cm.
DISTRIBUTION: Eurasia. Winters Afrotropical region and from southern Asia, Indonesia to northern Australia. HABITAT: Chiefly natural shallow

flooded grasslands or swampy standing water by rivers or margins of lakes. Outside breeding season mainly by lakes and rivers, flooded plains. FOOD: Chiefly invertebrates, sometimes fish. STATUS: Annual SV. [White-winged Tern]

Whiskered Tern
Chlidonias hybridus (Hydrochelidon hybrida). 23-25cm.
DISTRIBUTION: Palearctic, Southern Eurasia, India, south-eastern Asia, eastern and southern Africa and Australia. Winters in Africa and from southern Asia south to Sri Lanka, Indonesia, Australian region. HABITAT: By or on freshwater lakes, marshes, fish ponds. Outside breeding season mainly coastal waters and inland flooded areas and marshes. FOOD: Chiefly insects and larvae, also fish and amphibians. STATUS: SV.

Gull-billed Tern
Sterna nilotica (Sterna Anglica). 35-38cm.
DISTRIBUTION: Discontinuously in southern Palearctic, Australia and south-western Nearctic. Winters in tropical Africa, from southern Asia to Indonesia and Australasian region, and from southern USA south to southern South America. HABITAT: Sand-dunes, islands, shores of coastal and inland wetlands and pastures. In winter also on arable fields, marshes, beaches, lakes,rivers. FOOD: Varied diet including vertebrates and invertebrates. STATUS: CB (1950 and possibly 1949), regular SV.

Caspian Tern
Sterna caspia. 47-54cm.
DISTRIBUTION: Discontinuously in Eurasia,African region, southern Asia, Australia, New Zealand and North America. Winters coasts of continental Europe south to Africa, and southern Asia, USA to Central America. HABITAT: Coastal salt or freshwater lagoons and islets. Outside breeding season also inland marshes, waterways. FOOD: Mainly fish, some invertebrates. STATUS: Regular SV.

Sooty Tern
Sterna fuscata (Sterna fuliginosa). 33-36cm.
DISTRIBUTION: Widespread breeder in tropical and sub-tropical zones of Atlantic, Indian and Pacific Oceans. Outside breeding season ranges at sea in tropical Oceans. HABITAT: On oceanic islands. FOOD: Mainly fish. STATUS: SV.

—————————— PLATE 71 ——————————

Sandwich Tern
Sterna sandvicensis (Sterna cantiaca). 36-41cm.
DISTRIBUTION: Mainly north-western and southeastern USA, West Indies, northern and eastern coasts of South America. Winters Atlantic seaboard of Africa, Mediterranean and Persian Gulf; eastern coast of South America. HABITAT: Mainly sand or shingle beaches, sand-dunes, rocky islets. Outside the breeding season coastlines with mudflats, sandy beaches and rocky shores. FOOD: Chiefly fish. STATUS: MB, PV and SV (S.s.acuflavida).

Roseate Tern
Sterna dougallii. 33-38cm.
DISTRIBUTION: North-western Europe, Azores, east and south African region, southern Asia, Malayan Archipelago, Australia; eastern North America and West Indies. Winter south to western, eastern and southern Africa, across to Australia; south to northern South America. HABITAT: Maritime coast sites, especially islands. Mostly pelagic outside breeding season. FOOD: Chiefly marine fish. STATUS: MB (small numbers, 72 pairs 1995) and PV. **UK Red Listed.**

Common Tern
Sterna hirundo (Sterna fluviatilis). 31-35cm.
DISTRIBUTION: Palearctic, North America and West Indies. Winters mainly along coasts south of breeding range and as far south as southern Africa, southern South America and south-eastern Australia. HABITAT: Open shingle or sand beaches or spits, rocky islands or coasts, salt-marshes, also in some areas, inland. In winter mainly coastal. FOOD: Chiefly fish, also crustaceans. STATUS: MB and PV.

Arctic Tern
Sterna paradisaea (Sterna macrura). 33-35cm.
DISTRIBUTION: Northern Palearctic and northern North America. Winters in sub-Antarctic and Antarctic waters. HABITAT: Coastal and inshore islands, also inland. In winter mostly pelagic. FOOD: Mainly fish, crustaceans and insects. STATUS: MB and PV.

Little Tern
Sterna albifrons (Sterna minuta). 22-24cm.
DISTRIBUTION: Palearctic, southern Asia, Malayan Archipelagos and Australasia. Winters from southern Europe, southern Asia and Micronesia south to southern Africa and Australia. HABITAT: Prefers bare shingle, shell-beach or sand above tide or flood limits, coastal and inland. Outside breeding season, mainly marine. FOOD: Small fish and invertebrates, especially crustaceans and insects. STATUS: MB (small numbers) and PV.

—————————— PLATE 72 ——————————

Sabine's Gull
Larus sabini (Xema sabinii). 27-32cm.
DISTRIBUTION: Northern Palearctic and northern North America. Winters at sea in tropical eastern Pacific and Atlantic oceans. HABITAT: Coastal marshy flat tundra, floodlands, or shallow brackish pools. Rest of year pelagic; infrequently inland or coastal. FOOD: Invertebrates and small fish. STATUS: Scarce, regular PV, mostly autumn. [*Xema sabini*]

Ross's Gull
Rhodostethia rosea. 29-31cm.
DISTRIBUTION: Northern Palearctic and occasionally northern North America. Winter range unconfirmed; presumed to be along ice edge of Arctic Ocean. HABITAT: Along Arctic coast on swampy tundra. Rest of year pelagic. FOOD: Chiefly insects when breeding, elsewhere probably invertebrates and fish. STATUS: Irregular SV.

Bonaparte's Gull
Larus philadelphia. 28-30cm.
DISTRIBUTION: Northern North America. Winters in western, central and southern North America south to central Mexico and West Indies. HABITAT: Ponds or lakes in swampy areas with spruce Picea and tamaracks Larix. Outside breeding season moves to coasts, salt-marshes and mudflats, and inland lakes. FOOD: Invertebrates and fish. STATUS: Irregular SV.

Little Gull
Larus minutus. 25-27cm.
DISTRIBUTION: Northern Eurasia and northeastern North America. Winters south to Mediterranean region and Persian Gulf, and in North America in Great Lakes and along Atlantic coast of USA. HABITAT: Lowland freshwater wetlands or along coasts. Winters in offshore waters, along coasts and among coastal wetlands. FOOD: Invertebrates, especially insects, also fish; in winter, probably chiefly fish and marine invertebrates. Status: CB (0-1 pairs, 1989-93), regular PV and scarce WV.

Black-headed Gull
Larus ridibundus. 34-37cm.
DISTRIBUTION: Northern Palearctic and locally in northeastern North America. Winters south to central Africa, southern Asia, Philippines and Palau; from Great Lakes and Labrador south to Florida. HABITAT:

Inland and coastal marshes, moorland bogs, lakes, dunes, aquatic artefacts; in winter also inshore tidal waters, farmlands, rubbish dumps, urban parks. FOOD: Mostly animal material, especially earthworms and insects, also plant material, household and industrial waste. STATUS: RB, MB, PV and WV. Common and widespread. [Common Black-headed Gull]

Mediterranean Gull (Mediterranean Black-headed Gull)
Larus melanocephalus. 36-38cm.
DISTRIBUTION: Locally and mainly in east and south-eastern Europe. Winters in the Mediterranean, Black Sea, the Atlantic and North Sea coasts of Europe, and the Baltic. HABITAT: Coastal or inland in the hinterland of steppe lakes, marshes and deltas. Outside breeding season moves to coasts. FOOD: Chiefly insects when breeding; at other times mainly fish and molluscs. STATUS: CB (13-22 pairs, 1989-93), and small numbers PV and WV.

Common Gull
Larus canus. 40-42cm.
DISTRIBUTION: Eurasia and north-western North America. Winters in western Europe south to 45_N, to north-east Africa, Persian Gulf, and south-east Asia to Japan and southern China, and coastal North America from Alaska to California. HABITAT: Sea-coast sites, also near lakes, rivers, on moorlands, bogs, marshes. FOOD: Chiefly invertebrates, also fish. STATUS: RB, MB, PV and WV. [Mew Gull]

—————— PLATE 73 ——————

Great Black-headed Gull
Larus ichthyaetus. 57-61cm.
DISTRIBUTION: South-central Eurasia. Winters from eastern Mediterranean and Red seas, Persian Gulf and eastwards to south Asia. HABITAT: Shores and islands of inland seas and salt lakes, in winter sea-coasts. FOOD: Chiefly fish, mammals and insects. STATUS: SV (one record 1859). [Pallas's Gull]

Herring Gull (Herring-Gull)
Larus argentatus. 55-67cm.
DISTRIBUTION: Northern Eurasia and northern, central and eastern North America. Resident or dispersive; migratory populations move south to Mediterranean, (north-eastern Africa, Persian Gulf) southern Asia,and Gulf of Mexico. HABITAT: Sea-coast and inland sites, also on buildings; range over wide variety of habitats, marine, freshwater [in diverse and omnivorous diet. STATUS: Common RB, PV and WV. SV (*L.a.smithsonianus*).

Lesser Black-backed Gull
Larus fuscus. 52-57cm.
DISTRIBUTION: North-western and central-northern Eurasia. Winters mainly from Britain, Mediterranean, Black Sea, Turkmeniya and Persian Gulf to Arabian Sea and Afrotropic coasts. HABITAT: Dunes, shingle, cliffs, buildings, moors, bogs. Outside breeding season inland and marine, inshore or offshore. FOOD: Omnivorous, including garbage. STATUS: Chiefly MB and some RB and PV.

Iceland Gull
Larus glaucoides (Larus leucopterus). 52-60cm.
DISTRIBUTION: Southern Baffin Island and extreme north-west Quebec, and Greenland. Migratory to dispersive; wintering mainly on Atlantic coasts from Labrador to New England, and from eastern Greenland to Iceland, Faeroes and north-western Europe. HABITAT: Rocky coasts in fjords and sounds, normally on high cliffs. Outside breeding season in similar coastal waters. FOOD: Mainly fish. STATUS: Scarce WV, and SV (*L.g.kumlieni*).

—————— PLATE 74 ——————

Great Black-backed Gull
Larus marinus. 64-78cm.
DISTRIBUTION: Northern Atlantic coasts from eastern North America to coasts of northern Scandinavia and Russia. Migratory and dispersive; main European winter range south to Bay of Biscay and south-western Spain and American winter range south to Great Lakes and Florida. HABITAT: Coastal islands, islets and tops of stacks, also inland on lake islands and moorland. Outside breeding season mainly in offshore zone. FOOD: Omnivorous. STATUS: RB and WV.

Glaucous Gull
Larus hyperboreus (Larus glaucus). 62-68cm.
DISTRIBUTION: Palearctic and northern North America. Migratory to dispersive; wintering within or south of breeding range, or on coasts of eastern Asia south to Japan, and Aleutians to California. HABITAT: Coastal islands and cliffs, also sometimes inland. Outside breeding season mainly on sea-coasts, bays and harbours. FOOD: Omnivorous, animal material principally. STATUS: WV, most Scotland.

Kittiwake
Rissa tridactyla. 38-40cm.
DISTRIBUTION: Northern Palearctic and north-western and north-eastern North America. Winters south to Mediterranean region, Japan, north-western Mexico, north-eastern North America. HABITAT: Mainly high cliffs, locally on buildings. Outside breeding season largely pelagic. FOOD: Mainly marine fish and invertebrates. STATUS: RB and MB and few PV and WV. [Black-legged Kittiwake]

Ivory Gull
Pagophila eburnea. 40-43cm.
DISTRIBUTION: Northern Arctic Palearctic and Arctic North America. Winters south to northern Europe and northern Canada. HABITAT: High Arctic on ground, on steep cliffs or peaks above ice. Edge of pack-ice and glacier fronts, also scavenges. FOOD: Mainly fish and small marine invertebrates. STATUS: Irregular SV.

—————— PLATE 75 ——————

Great Skua
Catharacta skua (Megalestris catarrhactes). 55-58cm.
DISTRIBUTION: North-western Europe. Ranges at sea in northern Atlantic south to Britain to western Mediterranean and the Tropics. HABITAT: Coastal moorlands, grasslands and tundra. Pelagic outside breeding season. FOOD: Mainly fish, also birds, eggs, mammals, offal, carrion. STATUS: MB (Scotland) and PV.

Pomarine Skua (Pomatorhine Skua)
Stercorarius pomarinus (Stercorarius pomatorhinus). 46-51cm.
DISTRIBUTION: Northern Paleartcic and northern North America. Winters at sea mainly in low-latitude tropical seas. HABITAT: Coastal tundra and inland on tundra lakes and rivers. Outside breeding season pelagic. FOOD: Whilst nesting, chiefly lemmings, also eggs and young of birds. At other times chiefly fish. STATUS: Uncommon but regular PV.

Arctic Skua (Richardson's Skua)
Stercorarius parasiticus (Stercorarius crepidatus). 41-46cm.
DISTRIBUTION: Northern Palearctic and northern North America. Winters at sea south to southern South America and Africa, Australia and New Zealand. HABITAT: Predominantly coastal tundra, moorlands, and inshore islands. Outside breeding season primarily pelagic and along sea-coasts. FOOD: Chiefly fish; nesting birds away from the coast take birds, small mammals, insects and berries. STATUS: MB (Scotland) and PV.[Parasitic Jaeger]

Long-tailed Skua (Long-tailed or Buffon's Skua)
Stercorarius longicaudus (Stercorarius parasiticus). 48-53cm.
DISTRIBUTION: Northern Palearctic and northern North America. Winters at sea mostly in South Pacific and South Atlantic oceans off coasts of South America and south-western Africa. HABITAT: Arctic flat coastal tundra, stony plateaux to vegetated upland tundra. Outside breeding season pelagic. FOOD: When breeding, chiefly small rodents. At other times mainly fish, also offal and carrion. STATUS: Scarce but regular PV. [Long-tailed Jaeger]

PLATE 76

Razorbill
Alca torda. 37-39cm.
DISTRIBUTION: North-western Paleartcic and north-eastern North America. Winters offshore from breeding grounds in North Atlantic south to Florida, and western Mediterranean zone and Morocco. HABITAT: Coastal cliffs and boulder-strewn shores and islands. Outside breeding pelagic and along sea-coasts. FOOD: Chiefly fish, some invertebrates. STATUS: RB, MB and WV.

Great Auk
Pinguinus impennis (Alca impennis).
Extinct since 1844, when last pair killed on Eldey (Iceland). DISTRIBUTION: Bred formerly in North Atlantic region. Wintered at sea south to South Carolina and northern Europe. HABITAT: Colonial on small rocky islands with shelving access to sea. FOOD: Unknown, probably mainly fish.

Guillemot
(Common Guillemot) Uria aalge (Uria troile). 38-41cm.
DISTRIBUTION: Northern Palearctic, western and eastern North America. Winters at sea mostly near breeding gounds, ranging south to northern and north-western Europe, Japan, California and Virginia. HABITAT: Coastal cliffs. Pelagic and along sea-coasts. FOOD: Chiefly fish, some invertebrates. STATUS: RB, MB and WV; SV (*U.a.hyperborea*). [Common Murre or Common Guillemot]

Brünnich's Guillemot
Uria lomvia (Uria bruennichi). 39-43cm.
DISTRIBUTION: Northern Palearctic and northern North America. Winters at sea south to Norway, northern Japan, southern Alaska and New England. HABITAT: Coastal cliffs and rocky islands. Pelagic and along sea-coasts. FOOD: Chiefly fish, some invertebrates. STATUS: SV. [Thick-billed Murre]

Black Guillemot
Cepphus grylle (Uria grylle). 30-32cm.
DISTRIBUTION: Northern Palearctic, north-eastern and north-western North America. Winters at sea mostly near breeding grounds. HABITAT: Rocky islands, boulder-strewn coasts and low cliffs. At sea but usually in shallow waters. FOOD: Chiefly fish and marine invertebrates. STATUS: RB.

Little Auk
Alle alle (Mergulus alle). 17-19cm.
DISTRIBUTION: Northern Holarctic. Winters chiefly from Barents Sea westwards into Norwegian Sea, through Denmark Strait to Davis Strait and south to Grand Banks of Newfoundland. HABITAT: Boulder scree on Arctic islands. Pelagic and coastal waters. FOOD: Chiefly planktonic crustaceans. STATUS: Regular PV and WV; SV (A.a.polaris). [Dovekie]

Puffin
Fratercula arctica. 26-29cm.
DISTRIBUTION: North-western Palearctic and north-eastern North America. Disperses offshore from breeding sites and reaches south to Morocco and New Jersey. HABITAT: On islands and cliffs, in burrows, under boulders or in crevices in cliffs. Otherwise usually well out to sea. FOOD: Chiefly small fish, also marine invertebrates. STATUS: MB, RB, PV and WV. [Atlantic Puffin]

PLATE 77

Great Northern Diver
Gavia immer (Colymbus glacialis). 69-91cm.
DISTRIBUTION: North America and marginally western Palearctic. Winters mainly south of breeding range on Atlantic and Pacific coasts of Canada and USA, around British Isles and in North Sea. HABITAT: Chiefly on deep lakes in coniferous forest, scrub tundra or open tree-less areas. Winters mainly in coastal waters, some inland. FOOD: Mainly fish, some invertebrates. STATUS: CB (Scotland,1970 and possibly earlier), WV. [Common Loon]

White-billed Northern Diver
Gavia adamsii (Colymbus adamsi). 76-91cm.
DISTRIBUTION: Northern Eurasia and northern North America. Winters south of breeding range south to northern Norway, northern Japan and British Columbia. HABITAT: On standing or flowing water of tundra zone beyond tree-limit. Outside breeding season almost entirely at sea. FOOD: Mainly fish. STATUS: Regular SV. [Yellow-billed Loon]

Black-throated Diver
Gavia arctica (Colymbus arcticus). 58-73cm.
DISTRIBUTION: Eurasian Arctic and western Alaska. Winters south from southern edge of breeding range to the Mediterranean, Black Sea, south-eastern China and Japan. HABITAT: Deep lakes or extensive pools in tundra or coniferous forests. Outside breeding season chiefly in sheltered coastal marine areas. FOOD: Mainly fish. STATUS: MB or RB (Scotland, small numbers) and regular WV. [Arctic Loon]

Red-throated Diver
Gavia stellata (Colymbus septentrionalis). 53-69cm.
DISTRIBUTION: Northern Eurasia and northern North America. Winters on coasts from southern edge of breeding range south to Mediterranean, Japan, south-eastern China, and southern USA. HABITAT: Shallow pools, small lakes, promontories and islets. Outside breeding season moves to shallow inshore or coastal waters, some to inland lakes, large rivers. FOOD: Mainly fish. STATUS: MB and RB (small but increasing numbers), PV and WV. [Red-throated Loon]

PLATE 78

Great Crested Grebe
Podiceps cristatus. 46-51cm.
DISTRIBUTION: Palearctic, eastern and southern Africa, Australasia. Sedentary and migratory, Eurasian populations wintering south to Mediterranean region, northern India and south-eastern China. HABITAT: Fresh or brackish waters, natural or artificial, with open areas and fringed with vegetation. Winters on larger waters and sheltered estuaries and bays. FOOD: Chiefly fish, some invertebrates. STATUS: RB and WV.

Red-necked Grebe
Podiceps grisegena (Podiceps griseigena). 40-50cm.
DISTRIBUTION: Eurasia and North America. Winters mainly western Europe, Baltic, Caspian Sea and Mediterranean, both sides of the Pacific and in western USA to Gulf coast. HABITAT: Shallow, plant-fringed waters, usually inland. Outside breeding season moves to more open, often estuarine or coastal waters. FOOD: Mainly invertebrates, some fish. STATUS: CB (2 pairs, 1989-93), scarce WV; SV (*P.g.holboellii*).

Slavonian Grebe (or Horned Grebe)
Podiceps auritus. 31-38cm.
DISTRIBUTION: Northern Eurasia and North America. Winters to north-western Europe and south to Italy, Black and Caspian Seas, southern China, and southern USA. HABITAT: Usually shallow, small pools and lakes. Outside breeding season move mainly to inshore seas and large lakes. FOOD: Chiefly arthropods (especially insects), and fish. STATUS: RB (70-78 pairs, 1989-93) and WV. [Horned Grebe]

Black-necked Grebe (or Eared Grebe)
Podiceps nigricollis. 28-34cm.
DISTRIBUTION: Locally in Palearctic, and western North America, and eastern and southern Africa. Migratory and dispersive; winters south to Mediterranean region, northern Red Sea, Persian Gulf, northern India, southern China, southern Mexico and northern Central America. HABITAT: Small, shallow, well vegetated waters. Outside breeding season moves to open standing water or to sheltered estuaries, inshore shallows. FOOD: Chiefly insects, also molluscs, crustaceans, amphibians and fish. STATUS: MB or RB (23-48 pairs, 1989-93), PV and WV.

Little Grebe
Tachybaptus ruficollis (Podiceps fluviatilis). 25-29cm.
DISTRIBUTION: Eurasia, southern Asia, Malayan Archipelagos and New Guinea, and Africa south of Sahara. Mainly resident and dispersive, with some migration south within breeding range. HABITAT: Well vegetated ponds, lakes, rivers and reservoirs. Outside breeding season on more open waters and on coasts and estuaries. FOOD: Chiefly insects, molluscs, crustaceans, and fish. STATUS: RB, MB and WV.

———————————— PLATE 79 ————————————

Storm Petrel
Hydobates pelagicus (Procellaria pelagica). 14-18cm.
DISTRIBUTION: North-western Palearctic. Islands with rock crevices and burrows. Winters in eastern Atlantic from Scandinavia south to Mediterranean and southern Africa. HABITAT: Islands with rock crevices or burrows. Outside breeding season oceanic. FOOD: Plankton. small fish, offal. STATUS: MB. [European Storm-petrel]

Leach's Storm-petrel (Leach's Fork-tailed Petrel)
Oceanodroma leucorhoa (Oceanodroma leucorrhoa). 19-22cm.
DISTRIBUTION: Islands in Northern Pacific and northern Atlantic. Winters throughout eastern tropical Pacific and tropical Atlantic. HABITAT: Offshore islands with rock crevices or burrows. Outside breeding season at sea and off shore. FOOD: Chiefly plankton, small fish and offal. STATUS: MB and PV.

Madeiran Storm-petrel (Madeiran Fork-tailed Petrel)
Oceanodroma castro. 19-21cm.
DISTRIBUTION: Islands in subtropical and tropical Atlantic and Pacific Oceans. Disperses in winter at sea mainly within same region. HABITAT: In crevices and burrows. Otherwise at sea. FOOD: Chiefly crustaceans, fish and offal. STATUS: SV (1911 and 1931). [Band-rumped Storm-petrel]

Wilson's Storm-petrel (Wilson's Petrel)
Oceanites oceanicus. 15-19cm.
DISTRIBUTION: Islands of southern oceans and coasts of Antarctica. Migrates north to oceans ca. 47_N , wintering especially Atlantic and Indian Oceans. HABITAT: Rocky, remote islands, otherwise at sea. FOOD: Chiefly planktonic crustaceans, fish and offal. STATUS: SV.

White-faced Storm-petrel (Frigate-Petrel)
Pelagodroma marina. 20-21cm.
DISTRIBUTION: Islands of subtropical North Atlantic and southern

oceans. Migratory and dispersive; ranges at sea in Indian and Pacific oceans, and South Atlantic. HABITAT: Arid, undisturbed, small islands, in burrows. Otherwise pelagic. FOOD: Probably chiefly planktonic crustaceans. STATUS: SV (1897).

Great Shearwater
Puffinus gravis. 43-51cm.
DISTRIBUTION: Islands in South Atlantic Ocean. Ranges at sea in Atlantic north to Arctic Circle. HABITAT: Island burrows. Otherwise pelagic. FOOD: Mainly fish and squid. STATUS: Annual PV off coasts.

Sooty Shearwater
Puffinus griseus. 40-51cm.
DISTRIBUTION: On islands in south-eastern Australasian region and around southern South America. Ranges through most of southern oceans and moves to northern parts of the Pacific and Atlantic oceans. HABITAT: In burrows on islands. Otherwise pelagic. FOOD: Mainly squid, crustaceans and fish. STATUS: Annual PV.

Little Shearwater (Little Dusky Shearwater)
Puffinus assimilis. 25-30cm.
DISTRIBUTION: Islands in Atlantic and Australasian region. Disperses at sea outside breeding season. HABITAT: On islands in burrows and crevices. Otherwise pelagic. FOOD: Chiefly fish, crustaceans and cephalopods. STATUS: SV.

———————————— PLATE 80 ————————————

Manx Shearwater
Puffinus puffinus (Puffinus anglorum). 30-38cm.
DISTRIBUTION: Coastal regions of north-eastern Atlantic. Winter off eastern South America. HABITAT: Chiefly on inshore islands, in burrows. Oceanic but also often in nearshore areas outside breeding season. FOOD: Mainly fish. STATUS: MB.

Capped Petrel
Pterodroma hasitata (Oestrelata haesitata).
DISTRIBUTION: Haiti, Dominican Republic and Cuba, also probably Dominica. Ranges at sea in the Caribbean and off North American Atlantic seaboard. HABITAT: Breeding in burrows on inland cliffs. Otherwise pelagic. FOOD: Little information; probably fish, crustaceans and cephalopods. STATUS: SV (1850 and tideline corpse 1984. ***Global Conservation Concern***. [Black-capped Petrel]

Collared Petrel
Pterodroma brevipes (Oestrelata brevipes), one record, 1889 and Kermadec Petrel (Schlegel's Petrel) *Pterodroma neglecta (Oestrelata neglecta),* one record, 1908. Neither record now accepted in view of the improbability of these tropical and subtropical Pacific Ocean petrels occurring naturally in North Atlantic.

Bulwer's Petrel
Bulweria bulwerii. 26-28cm.
DISTRIBUTION: Islands of North Atlantic and Pacific between 40_N and 10_S. Winter south-west to tropical Atlantic. HABITAT: In holes or crevices. Outside breeding season pelagic. Squid, plankton and fish. STATUS: SV (1837, 1908, 1975).

Fulmar
Fulmarus glacialis. 45-50cm.
DISTRIBUTION: Northern Eurasia and northern North America. Migratory and dispersive; Wintering south to western Europe, Japan, Hawaiian Islands, California and south-eastern USA. HABITAT: Mainly on sea cliffs. Outside breeding season at sea. FOOD: Chiefly crustaceans, cepha-lopods, fish, offal and carrion. STATUS: RB, MB and PV. [Northern Fulmar]

Black-browed Albatross
Diomedea melanophris (Diomedia melanophrys). 80-95cm.
DISTRIBUTION: Islands of southern oceans. Migratory and dispersive; ranges at sea in southern oceans and north Atlantic to tropics. HABITAT: Remote oceanic islands on steep slopes and cliffs. Pelagic outside breeding season. FOOD: Mainly fish, crustaceans and molluscs. STATUS: SV.

--------------- PLATE 80A ---------------

Song Thrush (Hebridean Song-Thrush)
Turdus philomelos (Turdus hebridensis).
Now considered to be a race of the Song Thrush *T. p. hebridensis*, occurring in the Outer Hebrides and Isle of Skye (Scotland). See text Plate 1.

Wren (St Kilda Wren)
Troglodytes troglodytes (Troglodytes hirtensis).
Now considered to be a race of the Wren *T.t.hirtensi*s, occurring on St Kilda (Scotland). See text Plate 9.

Coal Tit (Irish Coal-Titmouse)
Parus ater (Parus hibernicus).
Now considered to be a race of the Coal Tit, *P.a.hibernicus*, occurring in Ireland. See text Plate 10.

Willow Tit (Willow-Titmouse)
Parus montanus (Parus kleinschmidti). 11.5cm.
DISTRIBUTION: Eurasia. Sedentary over much of range; some northern populations irregularly irruptive. HABITAT: Woodlands, coniferous, mixed and often swampy, also in winter, hedges, gardens, heaths and scrub. FOOD: Chiefly invertebrates in breeding season, with seeds and berries dominating in winter. STATUS: RB (*P.m.kleinschmidti*) and SV (*P.m.borealis*).

Marsh Tit (Marsh Titmouse) *Parus palustris*, see text plate 10

Redpoll (Greater Redpoll)
Carduelis flammea (Linota rostrata).
This appears to be the Greenland and Baffin Island race, *C.f.rostrata*, which occurs as a PV and WV to northern and western Scotland and probably bred in Inverness in 1959. See text plate 16.

Arctic Redpoll (Greenland Redpoll)
Carduelis hornemanni (Linota hornemanni). 13-15cm.
DISTRIBUTION: Northern Eurasia and northern North America. Partial migrant with irregular movements in winter south to the Baltic area, northern Mongolia and northern USA. HABITAT: Dwarf willows, birches, tundra and often on rocky ground. In winter on weedy fields. FOOD: Small seeds; some invertebrates in summer. STATUS: Irregular SV. [Hoary Redpoll]

--------------- PLATE 80B ---------------

Pied Wheatear (Eastern Pied Wheatear)
Oenanthe pleschanka (Saxicola pleschanka).
The first British specimen of a female of this rare vagrant, Isle of May, October 1909. See text plate 3.

Rüppell's Warbler
Sylvia rueppelli. 14cm.
DISTRIBUTION: South-western Eurasia in eastern Mediterranean region. Winters in north-eastern Africa (Chad and Sudan). HABITAT: Dry scrub on rocky hillsides and open oak forest with dense undergrowth. FOOD: Little information; insects and some fruit in autumn. STATUS: SV.

Moustached Warbler
Acrocephalus melanopogon (Lusciniola melanogopogon) 12-13cm.
DISTRIBUTION: Locally in southern Palearctic. Mainly resident or partially migratory to migratory; wintering from eastern Mediterranean region east to India. HABITAT: Reedbeds, sedges, dense vegetation near water, tamarisk thickets. FOOD: Chiefly arthropods, especially insects, spiders and molluscs. STATUS: CB (Cambridge, 1946) and SV.

Olivaceous Warbler
Hippolais pallida. 12-13.5cm.
DISTRIBUTION: Southern Palearctic, Sahara, Egypt and Arabia. Winters chiefly in tropical Africa. HABITAT: Breeds in riparian woods, scrub and woodland edges, also occurs in hedges, orchards, olive-groves, gardens and parks with trees and undergrowth. Winters in bushy steppe areas. Chiefly insects; also fruit in late summer. STATUS: Irregular SV.

Scottish Crossbill
Loxia scotica. 16-5cm.
DISTRIBUTION: Northern Scotland. Resident and dispersive. HABITAT: Primarily Caledonian Scots pine *Pinus sylvestris* forest and mature plantations with Scots pine. FOOD: Chiefly conifer seeds, primarily of Scots pine; some invertebrates in breeding season. STATUS: RB (350-1250 pairs, 1988). ***UK Red Listed. Global Conservation Concern.***

Pine Bunting
Emberiza leucocephalos (Emberiza leucocephala).
In winter plumage from the first British specimen, Fair Isle, 30th October 1911. See text plate 17.

Lesser Yellowlegs (Yellowshank)
Tringa flavipes (Totanus flavipes). 23-25cm.
DISTRIBUTION: Northern North America. Winters mostly from West Indies to South America, to Chile and Argentina. HABITAT: Grassy meadows, bogs and swampy muskeg. In winter on salt and fresh-water lagoons, tidal flats, brackish swamps and shallow open water. FOOD: Chiefly insects, also crustaceans, worms and small fish. STATUS: Regular SV.

INDEX

The numbers in italics after the listed name refer to the colour plate number.

Accentor, Alpine - *9*
Albatross, Black-browed - *80*
Auk, Great - *76*
   Little - *76*
Avocet - *64*

Bee-eater - *25*
Bittern - *41*
   Little - *41*
   American - *41*
Blackbird - *2*
Blackcap - *5*
Bluethroat - *4*
   White-spotted - *4*
Brambling - *16*
Bufflehead - *49*
Bullfinch - *17*
Bunting, Black-headed - *17*
   Cirl - *18*
   Corn - *17*
   Lapland - *18*
   Little - *18*
   Meadow - 18
   Ortolan - *18*
   Pine - *17/80B*
   Reed - *18*
   Rock - *18*
   Rustic - *18*
   Snow - *18*
Bustard, Great - *60*
   Little - *61*
Buzzard - *31*
   Honey - *35*
   Rough-legged - *31*

Capercaillie - *54*
Chaffinch - *16*
Chiffchaff - *6*
Chough - *19*
Coot - *59*
Cormorant - *39*
Corncrake - *59*
Courser, Cream-coloured - *62*
Crake, Little - *59*
   Spotted - *59*
Crane - *61*

Crossbill - *17*
   Two-barred - *17*
   Scottish - *80B*
Crow, Carrion/Hooded - *21*
Cuckoo - *25*
   Great Spotted - *25*
   Yellow-billed - *25*
Curlew - *69*
   Eskimo - *69*
   Slender-billed - *69*
   Stone - *61*

Dipper - *9*
Diver, Black-throated 77
   Great Northern - *77*
   Red-throated - *77*
   White-billed Northern - *77*
Dotterel - *62*
Dove, Rock - *53*
   Stock - *53*
   Turtle - *53*
Dowitcher, Short-billed - *68*
Duck, Ferruginous - *49*
   Harlequin - *50*
   Long-tailed - *49*
   Tufted - *4*
Dunlin - *66*
Dunnock - *9*

Eagle, Golden - *32*
   Spotted - *31*
   White-tailed - *33*
Eider - *50*
   King - *50*
   Steller's - *51*
Egret, Cattle - *40*
   Great White - *40*
   Little - *40*

Falcon, Gyr - *36-37*
   Red-footed - *38*
Fieldfare - *1*
Finch, Citril - *16*
   Snow - *17*
Firecrest - *9*
Flamingo, Greater - *42*
Flycatcher, Asian Brown - *14*
   Collared - *14*
   Pied - *14*
   Red-breasted - *14*
   Spotted - *14*
Fulmar - *80*

Garganey - *48*

Gadwall - *46*
Gannet, Northern - *39*
Godwit - *69*
   Bar-tailed - *69*
Goldeneye - *49*
Goldcrest - *9*
Goldfinch - *15*
Goosander - *52*
Goose, Barnacle - *44*
   Bean - *43*
   Brent - *44*
   Greylag - *43*
   Pink-footed - *43*
   Red-breasted - *44*
   Snow - *44*
   White-fronted - *43*
Goshawk - *34*
Grebe, Black-necked - *78*
   Great Crested - *78*
   Little - *78*
   Red-necked - *78*
   Slavonian - *78*
Greenfinch - *15*
Greenshank - *68*
Grosbeak, Pine - *17*
Grouse, Black - *55*
   Red - *55*
Guillemot - *76*
   Black - *76*
   Brünnich's - *76*
Gull, Black-headed - *72*
   Bonaparte's - *72*
   Common - *72*
   Great Black-backed - *74*
   Great Black-headed - *73*
   Herring - *73*
   Iceland - *73*
   Ivory - *74*
   Lesser Black-backed - *73*
   Little - *72*
   Mediterranean - *72*
   Ross's - *72*
   Sabine's - *72*

Harrier, Hen - *30*
   Marsh - *30*
   Montagu's - *30*
Hawfinch - *15*
Heron, Grey - *40*
   Night - *41*
   Purple - *40*
   Squacco - *41*
Hobby - *38*
Hoopoe - *25*

Ibis, Glossy - *41*

Jackdaw - *20*
Jay - *19*

Kestrel - *38*
   Lesser - *38*
Kildeer - *63*
Kingfisher - *24*
Kite, Black - *35*
   Red - *35*
Kittiwake - *74*
Knot - *66*

Lark, Crested - *22*
   Black – *22*
   Shore - *22*
   Short-toed - *22*
   White-winged - *22*
Linnet - *16*

Magpie - *20*
Mallard - *46*
Martin, House - *15*
   Sand - *15*
Merganser, Hooded - *52*
   Red-breasted - *52*
Merlin - *38*
Moorhen - *59*

Nightjar - *23*
   Egyptian - *23*
   Red-necked - *23*
Nightingale - *4*
   Thrush - *5*
Nutcracker - *19*
Nuthatch - *9*

Oriole, Golden - *14*
Osprey - *33*
Owl, Barn - *26*
   Eagle - *28*
   Hawk - *27*
   Little - *27*
   Long-eared - *26*
   Scops - *27*
   Short-eared - *26*
   Snowy - *27*
   Tawny - *26*
   Tengmalm's - *27*
Oystercatcher - *64*

Partridge, Grey - *58*
   Red-legged - *58*

Peregrine - 37
Petrel, Bulwer's - 80
  Capped - 80
  Collared - 80
  Storm - 79
  Storm-petrel, Leach's - 79
  Storm-petrel, Madeiran - 79
  Storm-petrel, White-faced - 79
Phalarope, Grey - 64
  Red-necked - 64
Pheasant - 57
  Chinese Ring-necked - 57
  Japanese - 57
  Mongolian - 57
Pintail - 47
Pipit, Meadow – 12
  Red-throated - 12
  Richard's - 12
  Tawny - 12
  Tree - 12
  Water - 12
Plover, Caspian - 62
  Golden - 63
  Grey - 63
  Kentish - 62
  Little Ringed - 2
  Pacific Golden - 63
  Ringed - 62
  Sociable - 63
Pochard - 48
  Red-crested - 48
Pratincole, Black-winged - 62
Ptarmigan - 56
Puffin - 76

Quail - 58

Rail, Water - 59
Raven - 20
Razorbill - 76
Redpoll - 16/80A
  Arctic - 80A
  Greenland - 80B
  Lesser - 16
  Mealy - 16
Redshank - 68
  Spotted - 68
Redstart - 4
  Black - 4
Redwing - 1
Ring Ouzel - 2
Robin - 4
Roller - 24

Rook - 21
Rosefinch, Common - 17
Ruff - 67

Sanderling - 66
Sandgrouse, Pallas's - 53
Sandpiper - 65
  Baird's - 65
  Buff-breasted - 67
  Common - 67
  Curlew - 66
  Green - 68
  Least - 66
  Marsh - 68
  Pectoral - 65
  Purple - 66
  Semipalmated - 67
  Solitary - 68
  Spotted - 67
  Terek - 65
  Upland - 67
  White-rumped - 66
  Wood - 67
Scaup, Greater - 49
Scoter, Common - 51
  Surf - 51
  Velvet - 51
Serin - 16
Shag - 39
Shoveler - 47
Siskin - 15
Shearwater, Great - 79
  Little - 79
  Manx - 80
  Sooty - 79
Shelduck, Common - 46
  Ruddy - 46
Shrike, Great Grey - 13
  Lesser Grey - 13
  Masked - 13
  Red-backed - 13
  Woodchat - 13
Skua, Arctic - 75
  Great - 75
  Long-tailed - 75
  Pomarine - 75
Skylark - 22
Spoonbill - 42
Starling - 19
  Rose-coloured - 19
Stork, Black - 42
  White - 42
Smew - 52
Snipe - 65
  Great - 65
  Jack - 65
Sora - 59

Sparrowhawk – 34
Sparrow, House - 16
  Tree - 16
Stilt, Black-winged - 64
Stint, Little - 66
  Temminck's - 66
Stonechat - 3
Swallow - 15
  Red-rumped - 15
Swan, Bewick's and
  Whistling Swan - 45
  Mute – 45
  Whooper - 45
Swift - 23
  Alpine - 23
  Needle-tailed - 23

Teal - 47
  Blue-winged - 47
  Green-winged - 47
Tern, Arctic - 71
  Black - 70
  Caspian - 70
  Gull-billed - 70
  Common - 71
  Gull-billed - 70
  Little - 71
  Roseate - 71
  Sandwich - 71
  Sooty - 70
  Whiskered - 70
  White-winged Black - 70
Thrush, Black-throated - 1
  Dusky - 2
  Mistle - 1
  Rock - 2
  Siberian - 2
  Song - 1/80A
  White's - 2
Tit, Bearded - 10
  Blue - 10
  Coal - 10/80A
  Crested - 10
  Great - 10
  Marsh - 10/80A
  Long-tailed - 10
  Willow - 80A
Treecreeper - 11
Twite - 17

Vulture,Egyptian - 29
  Griffon - 29

Wagtail, Blue-headed - 11
  Grey - 11

Grey-headed - 11
Pied or White - 11
White - 11
Yellow - 11
Yellow - 11
Wallcreeper - 11
Waxwing - 14
Wheatear - 3
  Isabelline - 3
  Black-eared - 3
  Desert - 3
  Pied - 3/80B
  Black - 3
Whimbrel - 69
Whinchat - 4
Whitethroat - 5
  Lesser - 5
Warbler, Orphean - 5
  Rüppell's - 80B
  Moustached – 80B
  Olivaceous – 80B
  Sardinian - 5
  Garden - 5
  Barred - 5
  Subalpine - 6
  Dartford – 6
  Yellow-browed - 6
  Pallas's - 6
  Willow - 6
  Wood - 6
  Radde's - 7
  Icterine - 7
  Melodious - 7
  Reed - 7
  Marsh - 7
  Great Reed - 8
  Sedge - 8
  Aquatic - 8
  Grasshopper - 8
  Savi's - 8
  Cetti's - 8
  Greenish - 6
Wigeon - 48
  American - 48
Woodcock - 65
Woodlark - 22
Woodpecker, Green - 24
  Great Spotted - 24
  Lesser Spotted - 24
Woodpigeon - 53
Wren - 9/80A
Wryneck - 24

Yellowhammer - 18
Yellowlegs
  Greater - 68
  Lesser - 80B